THE GOLF QUIZBOOK

Quarto

First published in 2024 by Ivy Press,
an imprint of The Quarto Group.
One Triptych Place,
London, SE1 9SH,
United Kingdom
T (0)20 7700 6700
www.Quarto.com

Every effort has been made to trace
the copyright holders of material
quoted in this book. If application
is made in writing to the publisher,
any omissions will be included in
future editions.

A catalogue record for this book is
available from the British Library.

ISBN 978-0-7112-9502-5
EBOOK ISBN 978-0-7112-9503-2

10 9 8 7 6 5 4 3 2 1

Design by Cara Rogers
Printed in China

MIX
Paper | Supporting
responsible forestry
FSC® C016973

THE GOLF QUIZBOOK

500 QUESTIONS TO TEST YOUR
GOLFING KNOWLEDGE

IVY PRESS

CONTENTS

INTRODUCTION

Golf can be a frustrating game at times, with nature, flag positions and sometimes your playing partner all conspiring to ruin a really great round. Golfers will be all too familiar with the unlucky bounce, the sudden gust of wind that steers a straight drive towards a water hazard, the giant divot a perfect drive nestles into, or your Titleist's magnetic attraction to badger droppings. Rest assured, none of that will happen within the pages of this quiz book. In fact to make things a little more like playing off a forward tee, most questions have multiple choice answers. This is in line with the R&A and the PGA philosophy that a round of golf should be played promptly.

There's a diverse range of questions to tax your golfing knowledge, from the major championships and the world's best players, to the rules of the game, interspersed by some of the more famous golf courses from around the world. Even if you don't know them, you can possibly guess which ones they are based on the landscape – especially if it's Utah or Iceland.

The book is split into 36 rounds/holes (two courses with one dogleg hole) plus a 19th hole at the end which includes some of the more diverse questions on the game, such as the drink that Arnold Palmer invented – or at least, gave his name to. Our favourite hole comes towards the end of the West Course and is a compilation of photographs of famous golfers when they were starting out, featuring a beardless Shane Lowry, Brian Harman with hair and Rickie Fowler doing a passable impersonation of 1970's teen idol David Cassidy.

Before you take to the first tee of the East Course, a word of warning from the committee – the accompanying pictures to some of the questions are not a 'gimme'. They may well be illustrating one of the multiple choice answers, but it's not a given that the picture is the correct answer. In our opinion, you can never have enough photos of Colin Montgomerie in a book, but sometimes other golfers were added to balance things up. Also, please be advised that the cut-off date for golf statistics from the majors is up to the Open Championship of 2023.

'And now, on the first tee...'

Hankley Common Golf Club, Surrey, England

EAST COURSE:
THE FRONT NINE

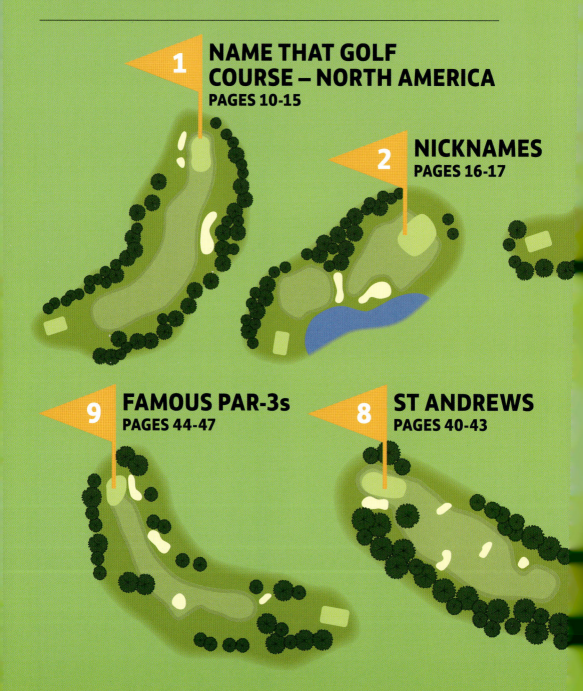

1 NAME THAT GOLF
COURSE – NORTH AMERICA
PAGES 10-15

2 NICKNAMES
PAGES 16-17

9 FAMOUS PAR-3s
PAGES 44-47

8 ST ANDREWS
PAGES 40-43

HOLE 1
NAME THAT GOLF COURSE – NORTH AMERICA

Without question the breadth of golf courses across North America is the greatest in the world – from mountainous challenges in ski resorts, to desert oases irrigated by springs, to wind-blown links on the Pacific and Atlantic shores, there is every challenge that can be posed to a golfer. We have selected some of the more famous and identifiable of the best of the USA and Canada, see if you can put a number to a name.

HARBOUR TOWN LINKS, SOUTH CAROLINA
OCEAN COURSE, KIAWAH ISLAND, SOUTH
  CAROLINA
OAKMONT COUNTRY CLUB,
  PENNSYLVANIA
SHADOW CREEK, LAS VEGAS, NEVADA
STREAMSONG GOLF RESORT, FLORIDA

ARROWHEAD GOLF COURSE, COLORADO

AUGUSTA NATIONAL GOLF COURSE, GEORGIA

FAIRMONT BANFF SPRINGS GOLF COURSE, ALBERTA, CANADA

CHAMBERS BAY, WASHINGTON

PACIFIC DUNES, OREGON

PEBBLE BEACH, CALIFORNIA

TPC SAWGRASS, FLORIDA

BROOKLINE COUNTRY CLUB, MASSACHUSETTS

MOAB GOLF COURSE, UTAH

TORREY PINES, CALIFORNIA

WAIKOLUA, KAUAI, HAWAII

WHISTLER GOLF CLUB, BRITISH COLUMBIA, CANADA

WHISTLING STRAITS, WISCONSIN

HOLE 2
GOLFING NICKNAMES

Golfers pick up nicknames whether they like them or not. Some are complimentary, most are not. In the early days of rivalry between established star Arnold Palmer, and the young pretender Jack Nicklaus, Arnie supporters labelled Jack (who came from Columbus, Ohio) 'Ohio Fats' alluding to his then-chubby profile. Assembled below are 22 of the best known golfing nicknames, along with 22 professional golfers. Can you match them?

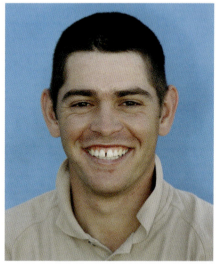

Louis Oosthuizen

1	Wee Mac	**Graeme McDowell**
2	The Goose	**Colin Montgomerie**
3	Shrek	**James Joseph Waldorf**
4	The Walrus	**Paul Azinger**
5	The Great White Shark	**John Daly**
6	Beef	**Thomas Trent Weekley**
7	Lefty	**Rory McIlroy**
8	The Golden Bear	**David Duval**
9	Duffy	**Paula Creamer**
10	The King	**Craig Parry**
11	Wild Thing	**Gary Player**
12	Big Easy	**Ernie Els**
13	Boom Boom	**Arnold Palmer**
14	Mrs Doubtfire	**Masashi Ozaki**
15	Double D	**Jack Nicklaus**
16	Popeye	**Greg Norman**
17	Jumbo	**Phil Mickelson**
18	Pink Panther	**Craig Stadler**
19	Big Mac	**Andrew Johnston**
20	Zinger	**Luis Ooosthuizen**
21	Boo	**Fred Couples**
22	The Black Knight	**Retief Goosen**

Craig Stadler enjoying the mud in 1990

Tiger Woods and Fred Couples at Augusta National Golf Club during the 2023 Masters Tournament

Graeme McDowell

Colin Montgomerie

HOLE 3
BALLS

The evolution of the golf ball has helped bring the sport to the masses. Once they were so expensive, only nobility and the gentry of Scotland could afford them. Nowadays they are so disposable that golfers stand on the shores of famous locks and wallop them into open water...

1 Until the arrival of the 'featherie' golf ball, players had to go out on the links with balls made out of what...?

a) Sandstone
b) Jute
c) Wood

2 Around 1618 a new type of golf ball was created by stuffing a cowhide sphere full of boiled feathers. Both leather and feathers were still wet when they were stitched together and as the leather shrank while drying, the feathers expanded to create a compact ball. The ballmakers would paint them white and stamp their name on them, such as Tom Morris or Allan Robertson. What kind of feathers did they use?

a) Grouse
b) Duck
c) Goose

3 Despite their rudimentary construction, featherie balls could travel some distance. A test was organized in Glasgow in 1786 and five drives by John Gibson averaged out at 193 yards. The Bryson DeChambeau of his day – Samuel Messieux – set the record for the longest drive with a featherie in 1836 at St Andrews. Although it was wind assisted it flew how far?

a) 247 yards
b) 306 yards
c) 361 yards

4 Featherie balls were fearsomely expensive, a skilled ballmaker could make just three or four in a day, and they came apart very easily. Golf was very much a rich man's game until the arrival of the gutta percha ball invented in 1848 by Robert Adams Paterson. It was created using a rubber-like latex from the tree *palaquium gutta* known as guttah (latex) percha (Sumatra). What was Paterson's occupation?

a) He was a Member of Parliament for Fife
b) He was an apprentice to ballmaker Allan Robertson
c) He was a divinity student at St Andrews University

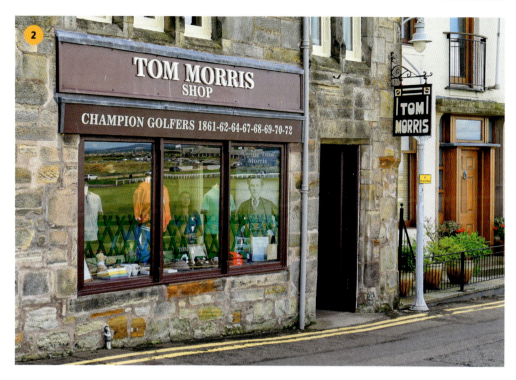

5 It was soon discovered that new, smooth-coated 'gutties' didn't fly as straight as ones that had a few nicks in the surface, so boys were employed to take a hammer and put blemishes in them, producing a 'hammered gutty'. True or False?

6 Golf truly became a sport for the masses with the advent of the rubber core golf ball invented by Coburn Haskell. This was a ball with a solid rubber core, high tension rubber thread wrapped around that core, and a gutta percha cover. Which American tyre company did he work for?

a) BF Goodrich
b) Firestone
c) Goodyear

7 Haskell balls, as they were known, were stamped with mesh, reverse mesh and Bramble designs. When did dimples first appear on golf balls?

a) 1905
b) 1921
c) 1927

8 Which make of golf ball is associated with James Bond films after the 1964 film in which Bond – played by Sean Connery – plays a round with Auric Goldfinger at the Stoke Park course (and actually switches balls)?

a) Penfold Heart
b) Spalding Pro Flite
c) Dunlop 65

9 Today, production of golf balls is a highly technical and lucrative business. Generally speaking, golfers should pick the compression of golf ball to suit their swing speed. If you have a slow swing speed (under 85mph) then it's best to go for high compression. True or False?

10 What was unusual about the Uniroyal Plus 6 golf ball (claimed to go six yards further than other golf balls) that was introduced in 1971?

a) It had hexagonal dimples
b) It had triangular dimples
c) It had circular and triangular dimples

11 Although balls have been white since the early days of golf, scientists believe that to avoid losing sight of a golf ball in flight, they would be better painted in which colour?

a) Red
b) Dark blue
c) Yellow

12 Which ball do most tour professionals play with?

a) TaylorMade TP5
b) Srixon Z-Star Diamond
c) Titleist ProV1

13 It has been estimated that golf balls could take between 100 and 1000 years to decompose, indeed gutta percha was used as the covering for the first transatlantic telegraph cables in the 19th century (dig up a vintage Haskell ball and it could be worth quite a bit). Despite having no golf courses on the shores of Loch Ness, in 2009 a sonar survey showed an estimated how many balls lying on the bottom of the loch?

a) 10,000
b) 50,000
c) 100,000

14 Tomorrow Golf is a sustainable golf business. How many golf balls do they estimate are lost by golfers every year?

a) 120-150 million
b) 200-230 million
c) 400-420 million

15 What is currently the most expensive golf ball on the market?

a) Titleist Pro V1X
b) Callaway Chrome Soft
c) Dixon Fire

HOLE 4
THE MASTERS

The fourth 'major' to be established, each Spring the Masters Tournament is eagerly awaited by golf fans the world over. The back nine of the Augusta National is a true test of a golfer's nerve and it is an irony that amidst the beauty of the azaleas and the impeccably prepared fairways, lie the ruins of many top golfer's major ambitions.

1 The original Augusta National designer, Alister MacKenzie, was a prolific golf course architect, born in Yorkshire of Scottish parents, who went on to design some of the world's greatest courses. Yet he trained as a surgeon and served in the Somerset Regiment working in field hospitals in which war?

a) Boer War
b) 1904 Sudan Revolt
c) World War I

2 Working before the age of massive earth-moving machinery, MacKenzie was sensitive to the natural contours of the land. The Augusta Country Club was one of his last few commissions; prior to that he had designed courses around the world. Which of the following was he not responsible for?

a) The Worcestershire Golf Club, England
b) Shinnecock Hills, New York
c) Royal Melbourne, Victoria, Australia
d) Cypress Point, California

3 MacKenzie died just two months before the initial Masters tournament (then known as the August National Invitational Tournament). When was that held?

a) 1928
b) 1934
c) 1938

4 Bobby Jones and Clifford Roberts had created the course at Augusta with the aim of hosting the US Open, but the USGA rejected it as a venue. What was the reason they gave?

a) The rail connections to Augusta were not adequate enough
b) There was not enough quality accommodation in the area to host officials and fans visiting the tournament
c) It would be too hot in Georgia at the traditional calendar date of the US Open

5 In the event of a tie in the 1930s (when there were no TV schedules to accommodate), the playoff would be held the following day. How many holes did they play

a) Nine
b) Eighteen
c) Thirty-six

The 15th green at Augusta. Patrick Reed believes it's the hardest par-5 on the course.

6 What Augusta tradition started in 1949?

a) The award of the green jacket
b) The pre-tournament par-3 competition
c) The oldest competitor acting as honorary starter

7 Zach Johnson (winner in 2007) is a big fan of the Augusta sand. 'You can't necessarily spin it a ton, but it's pure. You won't see a ball plug. Ever. It'll hit the bank and go back to the middle of the bunker or go through it.' Where does it come from?

a) It's Spruce Pine Sand from Western North Carolina
b) It's Bahamian Coral Sand from Grand Bahama

8 No golfer who has won the pre-tournament par-3 competition has ever gone on to win the Masters. Where is this held?

a) On the par-3 holes of the Augusta National
b) A special nine-hole par-3 course on the grounds
c) On the par-3 holes of the Augusta National, plus adapted tees playing to par-4 greens

9 The par-3 competition is a less formal event – who gets to caddy?

a) Players must choose one of their fellow competitors – it's only nine holes
b) Friends or family
c) Forces veterans

10 Past winners of the Masters are technically eligible to play in the competition for how long?

a) Ten years
b) Twenty years
c) Their lifetime

11 Gary Player was the first non-US golfer to win the Masters, who was the next?

a) Tony Jacklin
b) Bernhard Langer
c) Seve Ballesteros

Mowers out in force in 2018

12 Who has won the most Masters titles?

a) Arnold Palmer
b) Jack Nicklaus
c) Tiger Woods

13 In 2017 who did Sergio Garcia beat in a playoff to win his first major title?

a) Lee Westwood
b) Danny Willett
c) Justin Rose

14 One of golf's most famous bridges helps frame the par-3 12th hole, 'Golden Bell'. Who is it dedicated to?

a) Ben Hogan
b) Sam Snead
c) Bobby Jones

15 After the attack on Pearl Harbor, the United States entered World War II in December 1941, which meant the cancellation of the 1942 Masters.
True or False?

16 Which three holes on the course make up the much-feared 'Amen Corner'?

a) 10th, 11th, 12th
b) 11th, 12th, 13th
c) 12th, 13th, 14th

17 Where does the winner of the Masters traditionally receive his much-admired Green Jacket?

a) The Palmer Cabin
b) The Captain's Cabin
c) The Butler Cabin

18 There were four British winners of the Masters in a row between 1988 and 1991 (with Nick Faldo winning twice). But who was the first of them to don the Green Jacket?

a) Ian Woosnam
b) Sandy Lyle
c) Nick Faldo

19 Who traditionally helps the winner slip into their exclusive jacket?

a) The current Miss Georgia
b) The President of Augusta National
c) The previous year's winner

20 Who holds the record for the biggest margin of victory at the Masters with a 12-stroke advantage after 72 holes?

a) Jack Nicklaus 1965
b) Ray Floyd 1976
c) Tiger Woods 1997

21 Who holds the record for the lowest 72-hole score at the Masters with a 268, which equates to a staggering -20?

a) Tiger Woods
b) Jordan Spieth
c) Dustin Johnson

22 The defending champion gets to choose the menu for the following year's Masters Dinner and they often choose dishes native to their country. Bernhard Langer chose Wiener schnitzel, Sandy Lyle introduced everyone to his native haggis, so what did Nick Faldo go for?

a) Sausage and mash
b) Fish and chips
c) Chicken tikka masala

23 It makes regular appearances on broadcasts from the Masters – which hole number is this one?

24 There are many facets that are unique to a Masters competition. The club used to insist that it was only their caddies who would be used for the tournament, but they still prescribe a single make of golf ball and players have to sign a sponsor waiver to that effect.
True or False?

25 Which veteran broadcaster has been described as 'the voice of the Masters'?

a) Peter Alliss
b) Jim Nantz
c) Gary Koch

26 Spectators at the Masters are both knowledgeable and respectful. What is expressly banned at Augusta, but allowed in other competitions?

a) Visible tattoos
b) Dressing in the national flag of a country
c) Mobile/Cell phones

HOLE 5
LEFTIES

Left-handed people have to endure a range of things that right-handed people take for granted – like smudging the ink they've just written on the page, or having to push – not pull – a ballpoint pen across a notepad. In tennis they have a slight edge and all the equipment is the same, but in golf, the development of young players is often hampered by the lack of quality left-handed equipment. In North America it's estimated that left-handers make up between five and seven per cent of golfers.

1 Phil Mickelson became the oldest major winner in history when he won the 2021 PGA Championship at the age of 50 years, 11 months, and 7 days. He is the most successful left-handed golfer of all time, but does he sign his scorecards with his right or left hand?

2 Veteran Kiwi golfer Bob Charles has won the World Matchplay Championship, finished second in the PGA Championship (1968), third in the US Open (1964, 1970), but he won the Open at Royal Lytham and St. Annes after a 36-hole play-off with Phil Rogers. What was the year?

a) 1963
b) 1966
c) 1971

3 Bubba Watson's first name is…?

a) Gerry
b) Larry
c) Warren

4 The Floridian was nicknamed 'Bubba' by his father after NFL defensive end Bubba Smith, who played in two Super Bowls and was better known for his role as police officer Moses Hightower in the *Police Academy* movie series. True or False?

5 Brian Harman's domination of the final two rounds at Royal Birkdale in 2023 was a ratings loser for American broadcaster NBC. They recorded the lowest viewing figures for a final round since 2015 – and that was held on a Monday. That didn't bother left-hooker Brian who is an avid hunter and celebrated in a local hickory smokehouse, drinking Guinness out of the claret jug. What was his nickname in the press that week?

a) 'The Beerhunter'
b) 'The Butcher of Hoylake'
c) 'The Test Card'

6 Left-handers won the Masters three times out of four between 2003 and 2006. Phil Mickelson won two of the titles, who won the third?

a) Steve Flesch
b) Mike Weir
c) Russ Cochran

7 Which renowned former golfer-turned-journalist once said this about the greatest lefty of all time: 'Watching Phil Mickelson play golf is like watching a drunk chasing a balloon near the edge of a cliff.'

a) David Feherty
b) Gary McCord
c) Peter Alliss

8 Lefty winners are an even greater rarity on the LPGA tour. In 2014 there were no left-handed players at all, let alone winners. Though she plays right-handed, Nelly Korda can hit the famous 17th island green at TPC Sawgrass with both a right-handed swing and a left-handed swing. True or False?

9 In Scotland it is a legal obligation for all driving ranges to provide at least one tee box set up specifically for a left-handed player. True or False?

10 Bubba Watson played a miraculous shot to win the 2012 Masters playoff. On the downhill 10th hole, Watson's ball landed deep in the woods on pine straw without a clear route to the green. Using a wedge, Bubba improvized a Seve-like recovery shot with 40 yards of hook which stopped fifteen feet from the hole. Who was the playoff against?

a) Louis Oosthuizen
b) Retief Goosen
c) Ernie Els

HOLE 6
COMMENTATOR QUOTES

The good ones can add so much to the great occasions of golf, and the bad ones can have you diving for the mute button. Sometime, you want to write down exactly what they've just said...

1 Henry Longhurst was a veteran broadcaster on UK and US television with a rich, whisky-soaked English accent that suggested more than the occasional trip to the 19th hole. He is remembered by American audiences for his commentary at the 16th hole of the Masters tournament. Whose 40-foot putt was he describing on the 16th in 1975: 'My my.... in all my life I have never seen a putt quite like that'.

a) Jack Nicklaus
b) Tom Weiskopf
c) Hale Irwin

2 Which golf commentator was banned from Augusta – and worse still had Tom Watson write an angry letter to the broadcaster saying he was a disgrace and should be sacked for describing the speed of the greens at the Masters thus: 'I am not saying the greens are fast, but it's like they have been bikini-waxed'.

a) Nick Faldo
b) Ben Crenshaw
c) Gary McCord

3 Former European tour player-turned-journalist David Feherty has never been one to hold back; either in describing his own demons, or the egos of major-winning golfers. Who is he describing here? 'He thinks he invented fitness because he used to do push-ups on the airplane. He's just upset because you can't win a major any more with a low, flat hook and a Napoleon complex.'

a) Gary Player
b) Lee Trevino
c) Jack Nicklaus

One of the few days when the crowd *didn't* want it to blow a gale at the Open Championship...

4 Which former Scottish golfer, is famous for his on-the-course analysis of pin positions and fairway conditions and really looks forward to Open Championships hosted in Sandwich, Kent. 'I like Royal St George's, which many people don't, because it's got a super-abundance of wildlife. As soon as you step into the rough you're going: "Hey, what was that?" Royal Birkdale is pretty good. If you're lucky you can see red squirrels there, maybe sand lizards, which are very rare.'

5 Whose swing was David Feherty describing when he said: 'It's like an octopus falling out of a tree.'

a) Larry Mize
b) Jim Furyk
c) Tom Kite

6 Long time NBC commentator and former PGA tour professional Dave Marr once described: 'Golf's three ugliest words' as... ?

a) 'Out of Bounds'
b) 'It's hooking left'
c) 'Still your shot'

7 Who was Peter Alliss describing when he said, 'Here comes the Walrus... More moving parts than a Rolex watch. Legend!'

a) Craig Stadler
b) Pat Perez
c) Darren Clarke

8 Peter Alliss was watching a golfer's warming up exercises before his round in the 2011 Open Championship and commented: 'He was the hula hula champion for Santander for many, many years... that's the movement of a young man ... it's all in the daily routine of a golf professional ... those footballers, they work hard but this fella, he's 47!' Who was he describing?

a) Miguel Ángel Jiménez
b) Angel Cabrera

9 Who was David Feherty describing with this barb: '(It's the) worst haircut I've ever seen in my life. And I've had a few bad ones. It looks like he has a divot over each ear.'

a) Cameron Smith
b) Ricky Fowler
c) John Daly

10 Who was Peter Alliss describing after this golfer hit an 81 at the 2002 Open Championship at Muirfield: "It's like turning up to hear Pavarotti sing and finding out he has laryngitis."

Peter Alliss with Jackie Stewart, Lee Trevino, Sean Connery and Max Faulkner

HOLE 7
SPANISH GOLFERS

When the game of golf spread across Europe in the post-war years, it was Spain that produced some of the greatest names to challenge for honours.

1 When Sergio Garcia burst onto the scene in 1999 after scoring the lowest amateur round in the Masters, what was his nickname?

a) El Torro
b) El Niño
c) Pequeño Seve (Little Seve)

2 Jon Rahm turned professional in 2016 and already has an extensive trophy room filled with awards from every phase of his career. Which are the first two majors that he's won?

a) Open Championship and US Open
b) Masters and PGA
c) Masters and US Open
d) Open Championship and PGA

3 When Sergio Garcia won the Masters, that made it how many Spanish victories in the tournament?

a) Three
b) Four
c) Five

4 Although he had been World Amateur Champion before, Jon Rahm really announced himself on the professional world stage in 2017 by winning the prestigious PGA event, the Farmers Insurance Open at Torrey Pines. Where was he on the World Rankings before that win?

a) 82
b) 137
c) 588

5 Miguel Ángel Jiménez was a familiar figure on the European circuit for two decades. What was he known for as he made his way round the course.

a) Constantly popping tic-tacs
b) Smoking a cigar
c) Chewing on a white plastic tee (which he never played off)

6 In which Spanish region would you find the Seve Ballesteros Airport?

a) Andalucia
b) Cantabria
c) Galicia

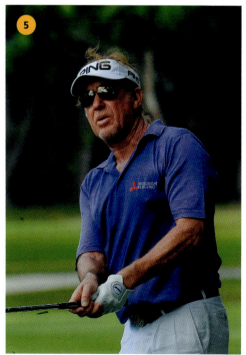

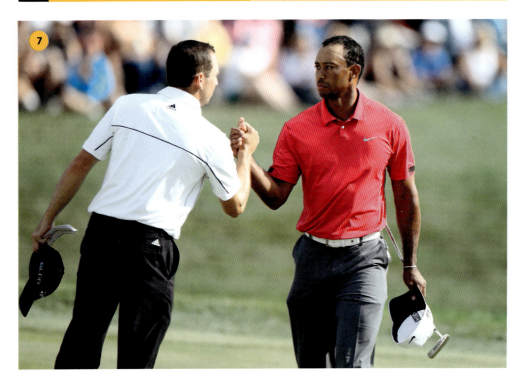

7 Sergio Garcia has never had the greatest relationship with Tiger Woods, a spat that rumbled on from 1999. At the 2006 Open Championship Tiger began the final round a stroke ahead of him and then beat him by six shots. Garcia was dressed all in yellow that day and allegedly Tiger texted a friend afterwards saying: 'I just bludgeoned Tweety Bird.' True or False?

8 Veteran Spanish golfer Miguel Ángel Jiménez joined the European tour in 1988. What record does 'The Mechanic' hold?

a) Most starts on the European tour
b) Most wins on the European tour
c) Most cuts missed on the European tour

9 Who won the Spanish Open golf tournament three consecutive times between 2019 and 2022 (2020 was cancelled)?

a) Jon Rahm
b) David Puig
c) Adrián Otaegui

10 Which of these professional golfers is not Spanish?

a) José María Cañizares
b) Manuel Piñero
c) Pablo Larrazábal
d) Edouard España

Panamera 4 E-Hybrid Sport Turismo
Hole in One

PORSCHE

11 Jon Rahm has many things in common with José María Olazábal, but which of the following is true?

a) As children they both wanted to follow in the footsteps of the great Spanish cyclist Miguel Induráin
b) They are both from the Basque Country
c) They are both directors of football club Athletic Club Bilbao

12 Can you name this moustachioed Spanish professional posing at the Benson and Hedges International Open Golf Tournament held at the St Mellion International Golf Resort, Cornwall?

HOLE 8
ST ANDREWS

St Andrews Old Course is officially the Oldest Golf Course in the World. For many years it was thought to be Musselburgh, indeed, that course has a Guinness Book of World Records plaque that proudly announces that it is the oldest golf course still being played. However, as more and more ancient documents are retrieved and deciphered from Scottish archives, the more we learn about: *Goff, gowf, golf, goif, goiff, gof, kolf, gowfe, gouff and golve*, as it's been recorded. These confirm that the *gowf* played on the Old Course was in the same area as it is played today.

1 The Captain of the Gentlemen Golfers, William St Clair of Roslin made some far-reaching changes to the course. Originally there were twenty-two holes at St Andrews but the Scottish feudal Baron decided that the first four and last four holes on the course were too short and should be combined. The result was eighteen holes and the template for all golf courses going forward (except in Prestwick where they had twelve). When was this change made?

a) 1621
b) 1764
c) 1831

2 Golf was banned in Scotland in 1457 because it was distracting young men from practicing martial skills, such as archery. King James IV effectively lifted the ban on golf in 1502 by buying his first set of clubs and, like all golfers ever since, kept on buying new clubs and balls. The purchases and the intention to play golf at St Andrews are recorded in royal accounts, but there was no documentation as to exactly where the links were at St Andrews. This came when?

a) In 1552, Archbishop John Hamilton of St Andrews was given a licence to establish a rabbit warren on the north part of the golf links
b) In 1567 Mary Stuart (Mary Queen of Scots) provoked gossip by 'playin o' the *gowf*' on St Andrews links when she should have been in mourning for her husband Lord Darnley
c) In 1588 the *El Gran Grifón*, a remnant of the Spanish Armada, was shipwrecked at St Andrews, an incident first reported by Dughaill Douglas 'observing o' the *goif* links'

3 Where will you find the Valley of Sin in St Andrews?

a) On the corner of Market Street behind the Albany Hotel
b) Just in front of the 18th green
c) Separating the 4th green and the 5th tee (a convenient relief point)

4 The Old Course only became the 'old' course in 1895 when the New Course was built. Because the course occupies common land, The Royal and Ancient Golf Club are not the only ones entitled to use the links of St Andrews, there are four other clubhouses nearby. True or False?

5 Who holds the record for the lowest aggregate score over four rounds at an Open Championship held on the Old Course – 268 strokes

a) Jack Nicklaus
b) Tiger Woods
c) Cameron Smith

6 Bobby Jones was an unashamed fan boy of St Andrews and the feeling was mutual. Jones said: 'If I had to select one course upon which to play the match of my life, I should have selected the Old Course.' In 1958 the mayor of St Andrews gave Jones the key to the city and he became only the second American to receive that honour. Who was the first?

a) Benjamin Franklin
b) Samuel Clemens (Mark Twain)
c) Franklin D. Roosevelt

7 Many of the 112 bunkers on the Old Course have names and stories behind those names. On the 16th hole there is the Deacon Sime bunker, a little further on from the Principal's Nose bunkers. How did it gets its name?

a) Deacon Sime was a keen golfer but rarely escaped this bunker in one stroke. When he finally did manage it and scored a par on the hole he declared it a miracle
b) His ashes were scattered in it. He argued that he'd spent so much time in it during his lifetime that it would be an appropriate place to spend eternity
c) He employed one of his parishioners with a West Highland Terrier to retrieve his ball whenever it landed there and drop it in a blind spot on the fairway before his playing partners arrived

8 The famous Swilcan/Swilken Bridge that golfers cross on the 18th fairway is thought to be how old?

a) 400 years
b) 700 years

9 'Miss Grainger's Bosoms' are two prominent mounds on the 15th hole. They are affectionately named after Agnes Grainger, a much-admired member of St Andrews Ladies Putting Club in the 19th century. It was said that Victorian golfers loved the sheer 'edginess' of mentioning Miss Grainger's Bosoms. Or have we just made this up? True or False?

10 There are no bunkers on the 1st and 18th holes on the Old Course. True or False?

11 Which golfer is missing from this sequence of Open winners on the Old Course?
2000 Tiger Woods
2005 Tiger Woods
2010 Louis Oosthuizen
2015
2022 Cameron Smith

a) Zach Johnson
b) Jason Day
c) Jordan Spieth

12 Who is the course record holder at St Andrews' Old Course – a round of 61 in 2017?

a) Rory McIlroy
b) Paul Lawrie
c) Ross Fisher

HOLE 9
FAMOUS PAR-3s

Par-3s should be a lot of fun – each time they present the opportunity for that once-in-a-lifetime hole in one (except if you're playing Oakmont). But they are fickle creatures, they may be full of promise, but they're normally surrounded by an array of hazards waiting to dash the average golfer's hopes. Here are some of the most treacherous...

1 At 123 yards, the 8th hole at Troon is a right royal tiddler. The 'Postage Stamp' is so-named because of its small green, which is heavily guarded by bunkers. Gene Sarazen judged the wind blowing in across the Firth of Clyde to perfection and scored a hole in one in 1973. It was a fitting final round in the Open for the seven-times major winner. When had he first played Troon (and failed to qualify)?

a) 1923
b) 1933
c) 1948

2 The 4th hole at Royal County Down in Northern Ireland offers breathtaking views across Dundrum Bay towards which range of mountains?

a) Mountains of Mourne
b) MacGillycuddy's Reeks
c) Ben Gourm Mountains

3 The course at Oakmont is a pretty stern test of golfing ability, none more so than the par-3 8th hole, the longest par-3 in US Open history when it was played from 300 yards in 2007. Organizers point out that it is in fact one of the longest and flattest greens on the course (...and it's surrounded by massive bunkers and a ditch). For the 2016 event they shortened it to a mere 299 yards. How many birdies were recorded across four rounds?

a) 3
b) 24
c) 37

4 The 12th at Augusta, looks unthreateningly beautiful, especially when the azaleas are in bloom, framed by two elegant bridges. At 155 yards it's not a long hole, in fact it's the shortest par-3 on the National course. But with the creek running in front and a lightning fast green and apron assisting a meeting of ball and water, it can be a score wrecker. Tommy Nakajima carded a 13 here at the 1978 Masters. Where does it rank in a table of most difficult holes at Augusta?

a) 1st
b) 4th
c) 6th

5 The challenge of the 16th hole on the Green Monkey Course at Sandy Lane is one of not being overawed by the experience. It plays 226-yards downhill into the depths of the towering quarries that have been reclaimed for the greatest game. Beyond the lengthy green is a vast expanse of water and in front of the green a vast expanse of sand with a large monkey-shaped island of grass, making it the signature hole. On which Caribbean island would you find Sandy Lane?

a) Jamaica
b) Antigua
c) Barbados

6 It's the poster boy for Pacific-coast golf, the 7th at Pebble Beach, with the manicured green nestled so close to the booming ocean surf is one of the most photographed holes in the world. At 111 yards it's even shorter than the Postage Stamp, but it's rarely without a sea breeze, and a sloping green doesn't make things easy. What part of the course is this called?

a) Arrowhead Point
b) Monterrey Point
c) Point Loma

7 The 16th hole at TPC Scottsdale wouldn't be out of place in Japan. The grandstand for the Waste Management Phoenix Open tournament completely surrounds the 163-yard par-3, and spectators have been known to enjoy a beer or seven. This raucous behaviour has gained it a nickname...

a) The Coliseum
b) The Bear Pit
c) The Ballpark

8 Whistling Straits has a testing 17th hole par-3 that can play to 249 yards from the furthest tee back or as little as 131 from the closest. The green is guarded left by a gaggle of sand dunes that are waiting for a tee shot 20 feet below green level, and a similar array above to the right. If a tee shot hooks beyond the bunkers to the left, Lake Michigan is there waiting. The hole has a name, what is it?

a) Pinched Nerve
b) Almost Home
c) Ramparts

9 The Ocean Course, Kiawah Island, has hosted both the US Open and the Ryder Cup and undoubtedly has one of the most challenging penultimate par-3 holes in the world. Measuring 223 yards, which can be into a stiff South Carolina breeze, this hole has water jeopardy short right, right and long right, so don't fade. It has bunkers left, so don't hook. It was designed by the same golf architect responsible for TPC Sawgrass (and there's another challenging 17th) – who is it?

a) Tom Doak
b) Pete Dye
c) Tom Fazio

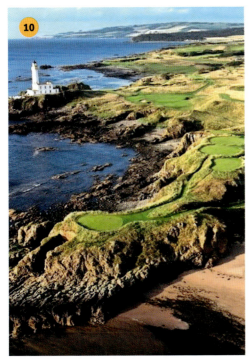

10

The teeshot at the 9th hole at Turnberry has always been one of the most challenging in golf. The back tee has its own rugged little promontory jutting into the sea, demanding golfers carry shots a good distance over the Ayrshire coastline. Even the forward tees involve shots that have to clear a couple of small coves. Despite the jeopardy, the view out to the Firth of Clyde, past the Turnberry lighthouse is almost worth the enormous green fee. How long is the hole?

a) 175 yards
b) 206 yards
c) 248 yards

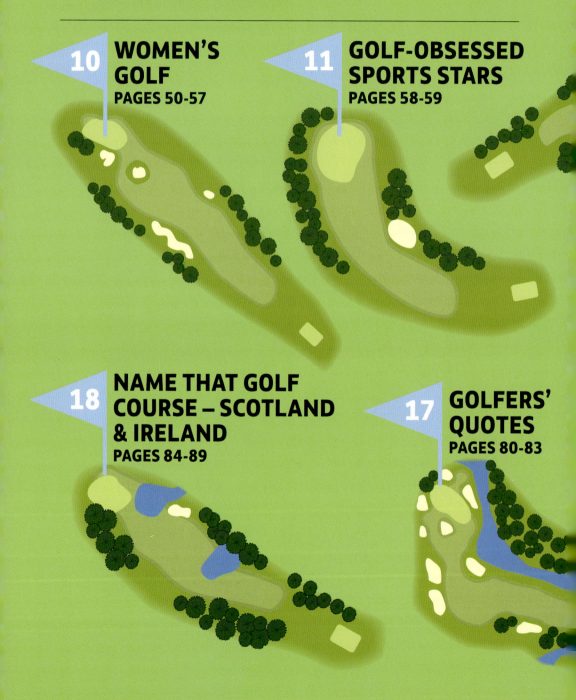

EAST COURSE:
THE BACK NINE

HOLE 10
WOMEN'S GOLF

Women's golf has come a long way since players were obliged to go onto the golf course in long, mud-collecting skirts, big flappy sleeves and wearing a straw boater held down by an industrial strength hatpin. Even so, May Hazlet, winner of the Ladies Championship in 1899, 1902 and 1907 decried the introduction of 'the shortest narrow bicycling skirts' where a calf or ankle might be glimpsed. Today, it's very different.

1 With hopeless men faffing around and failing to create a proper handicap system in golf, it was left to Issette Pearson the Honorary Secretary of the Ladies Golf Union to devise the first universally adopted handicap system. When was it first used?

a) 1893
b) 1912
c) 1923

2 As a 14-year-old in 2009, Lexi Thomson qualified for the U.S. Women's Open and made the cut finishing tied for 34th How many times had she played the event before that?

a) It was her debut
b) It was her second appearance
c) It was her third appearance

3 Lydia Ko was the Rolex LPGA Player of the Year in 2022. What nationality is Lydia?

a) Korean
b) Chinese
c) American
d) New Zealander

4 They start them young on the women's tour. Lydia Ko first won LPGA Player of the Year in 2015. For a short time in 2012 she held the record for the youngest person ever to win a professional golf tour event. She was edged out by Canadian golfer Brooke Henderson who won an event on the Canadian tour in June of that year. At what age?

a) 14
b) 15
c) 16

5 The LPGA elevated the Women's British Open to major status to replace the du Maurier Classic after the Canadian government restricted tobacco sponsorship. When did the British Women's Open first come into existence?

a) 1936
b) 1964
c) 1976

6 For a decade between 1995 and 2005 Swedish golfer Annika Sörenstam dominated the women's game. How many LPGA Player of the Year awards did she win in that time?

a) Six
b) Seven
c) Eight

7 Michelle Wie (now Wie-West) became the youngest player to qualify for a USGA amateur championship at what age?

a) Seven and a half
b) Ten
c) Twelve

8 There are five LPGA majors: The Chevron Championship, Women's PGA Championship, US Women's Open, The British Women's Open and the Evian Championship (Europe). Which courses host the Evian Championship?

a) Only one, at Evian Les Bains, France
b) Varies between courses in France, Italy, Germany and Sweden
c) Varies between courses in France, Switzerland, Austria, Sweden and Denmark

6

9 Pamela Barton was a top amateur golfer in England before World War II – her first big win was the French Amateur Championship in 1934 when she was 17. In 1936, she won both the British Ladies Amateur and the US Women's Amateur. She won the British Ladies again in 1939. Working for the RAF In World War II, she was killed in a plane crash at an airbase near Maidstone, Kent, in 1943. She is memorialized in two ways below – name the odd one out

a) The inner course at Royal Mid-Surrey, near Richmond, was named after her
b) There is a statue of her at the R&A in the St Andrews lobby
c) The British Ladies Amateur champion receives the Pam Barton Memorial Salver each year

10 At the 2013 US Women's Open Jessica Korda and caddy Jason Gilroyed had several disagreements, and after shooting 5-over-par for the front nine, she fired him on the spot. Who took over?

a) No-one, she slimmed her bag down to 11 clubs and carried them herself

b) A spectator

c) She called her boyfriend, professional golfer Johnny DelPrete, to come in from the gallery

11 What nationality is Minjee Lee?

a) American

b) Chinese

c) Belgian

d) Australian

12 Renee Powell, from Ohio, was only the second Black golfer to play on the LPGA tour and during her 14-year career played 250 professional tournaments. A student hall of residence at St Andrews University is named in her honour. In 2015 she became one of the first women members of the Royal and Ancient Golf Club of St Andrews. True or False?

13 England's Charley Hull turned professional at the age of 16 in 2013. She is 23 days older than her Solheim Cup team-mate Georgia Hall. Which of them won the 2018 British Women's Open?

a) Georgia Hall

b) Charley Hull

14 Team Great Britain and Ireland may have roped in the Europeans to take on the US in the men's Ryder Cup, but in the biennial women's amateur team competition, it's still the British Isles challenging the States. What is the competition called?

a) The Curtis Cup
b) The Mickey Walker Cup
c) The Nancy Lopez Trophy

15 Golf hadn't been included in the Olympic Games since 1900, for women, and 1904 for men. Who won the gold medal at Rio in 2016?

a) Lydia Ko
b) Shanshan Feng
c) Inbee Park

16 ...and five years later, at the Kasumigaseki Country Club, who won the gold medal at the delayed 2020 Tokyo Olympics?

a) Nelly Korda
b) Jessica Korda
c) Lydia Ko

17 Like many professional women's sports – soccer, cricket, rugby, cycling – golf is growing. The prize fund on offer by the LPGA in 2023 was the biggest ever. What was the figure?

a) $75m
b) $96m
c) $101m

18 In 2017 Lexi Thompson was on the wrong end of a terrible implementations of golf rules. Playing in the third round of the ANA Inspiration tournament she was adjudged to have incorrectly marked her ball by an inch on a one-foot putt. Despite being followed round by a rules official – who saw nothing wrong – the slip was witnessed by a TV viewer and emailed to the organizers. Lexi got a four-stroke penalty, two for the incorrect marking and two for signing her card without adding on those two strokes. When did she learn of her penalty?

a) Thirty minutes after she signed her third round card
b) Thirty minutes before she teed off the following day
c) Six holes before the end of the final round, when she was leading

19 Michelle Wie is the same height as Tiger Woods – True or False?

20 The women's equivalent to the Ryder Cup, played between the USA and Europe in exactly the same format, is the Solheim Cup. It was set up by Karsten Solheim, the Norwegian-American businessman behind Ping and, like the Ryder Cup, takes place biennially. When did it start?

a) 1976
b) 1982
c) 1990

HOLE 11
GOLF-OBSESSED SPORTS STARS

Many top sportsmen aren't content to trounce the opposition in their chosen sport, they have to take that competitive streak out onto the golf course too. Like this lot...

1 Which NBA basketball star scored a hole in one at the 2023 American Century Championship?

a) Steph Curry of the Golden State Warriors
b) LeBron James of the L.A. Lakers
c) Nikola Jokic of the Denver Nuggets

2 Manchester City manager Pep Guardiola has said that he is not going to stay in football management too long because he wants to reduce his golf handicap. Which European professional does he get the occasional lesson from?

a) Tommy Fleetwood
b) Jon Rahm
c) Viktor Hovland

3 Usain Bolt is a unique sportsman who, after winning three 100m Olympic sprints retired to his native Jamaica. One of the world's richest sportsmen, he has bought the Robert Trent Jones-designed course at Half Moon Bay, near Montego Bay, and reserves the tee time between 9am and 9:30am each day, should he want to play. True or False?

Lando Norris

Rafa Nadal and Sergio Garcia

4 Before his retirement, former Tottenham and Real Madrid footballer Gareth Bale was criticized by fans of the Spanish side. His nine-year tenure at Real Madrid was often dogged by soccer pundits who thought he was more committed to his golf clubs than his football club. After qualifying for Euro 2020 Bale's team-mates in the Welsh side held up a banner that read: "Wales. Golf. Madrid. In that order". True or False?

5 The American Century golf tournament is an annual event held on the shores of Lake Tahoe in California, featuring stars from other sports, and also Sweden's multiple women's champion Annika Sörenstam. There are many former and current NFL stars who take part, but who was the highest placed in 2023?

a) Tony Romo
b) John Elway
c) Aaron Rodgers

6 Two weeks after picking up his 22nd tennis grand slam win by defeating Casper Ruud at the French Open, Rafa Nadal turned his attention to the golfing challenge of the Balearic Championship in Mallorca. Nadal who plays between 0.3 and 1.5 finished where?

a) 5th
b) =21st
c) Last but one

7 With Nadal's recurring foot injury hampering his return to tournament play, he'll have time to develop his short game, like these former tennis players. Who is the best among them with a 0.5 handicap?

a) Pete Sampras
b) Ivan Lendl
c) Andy Roddick

8 Which Manchester United and England footballer took part in the LIV golf pro-am at Valderrama, partnered by sacked Ryder Cup captain Henrik Stenson (there's a certain synchronicity here)?

a) Harry Maguire
b) Luke Shaw
c) Marcus Rashford

9 McLaren Formula 1 driver Lando Norris once described golf as: 'the most boring thing ever'. Then a team-mate took him for a round of golf and he saw the light. Who was that driver?

a) Daniel Ricciardo
b) Carlos Sainz
c) Fernando Alonso

10 Which Super Bowl-winning quarterback loves golf so much he has just had a par-3 hole and large green constructed in his back garden?

a) Patrick Mahomes
b) Josh Allen
c) Jared Goff

HOLE 12
RULES, RULES, RULES

There are a lot of rules in golf, especially for people who only occasionally visit a fairway. You can't hit a ball that isn't yours. But when you find a ball deep in the rough, if you try too hard to identify it you can be accused of improving your lie or causing it to move. And that's just bash-it-about club golf; the professionals have it a lot worse. Try and see if you can steer the right side of these golf rules...

1 If, when the ball is dropped, the ball rolls out of the relief area, what happens next?

a) Providing the drop took place within the relief area, then play can continue with no penalty
b) The ball must be dropped again until it remains in the relief area

2 Following the change of rules introduced by the R&A and the USGA in 2019, a dropped ball in a relief area must be made from...

a) Knee height
b) Hip height
c) Shoulder height

3 You can't tee off in front of the tee markers, but how far behind the line can you tee off?

a) As far back as there is tee grass
b) One club length
c) Two club lengths

4 In tournament play, how long are you allowed to search for a lost ball?

a) Three minutes
b) Four minutes
c) Five minutes

5 What is the maximum number of clubs allowed in a golf bag?

a) 13
b) 14
c) 14 and a putter

6 You hit a putt that hovers on the lip of the hole, teetering on the edge, held up by a couple of stubborn blades of grass. How long are you allowed to wait for it to take a chance gust of wind and drop?

a) 20 seconds

b) 10 seconds

c) 10 seconds from when you arrive at the hole to see just how close it is

7 Does the status of an area marked Ground Under Repair (GUR) count exactly the same as a lateral hazard? Yes/No

8 A golfer finds his ball in the deep rough, hacks it out onto the fairway, then realises it's not his ball. If he takes a 2-stroke penalty for playing the wrong ball, is he allowed to continue with that ball - given that the rules of golf are weighted towards prompt play? Yes/No

9 If you chip a ball and it holes out, wedged between the flag and the side of the cup, with some of it still showing above the putting surface, is that considered holed – a situation Shawn Stefani encountered in 2013 when he hit a fortuitous hole in one on Merion's par-3 17th hole. Yes/No

10 Previously, if you were putting and left the flagstick in – and then hit it with your putt – that resulted in a two-stroke penalty. What has this been reduced to?

a) One stroke penalty
b) No penalty

11 If you hit a tree that is clearly out of bounds and it takes a lucky bounce back onto the fairway, is that considered Out of Bounds? Yes/No

12 Is there a penalty for playing out of turn in stroke play? Yes/No

13 Is there a penalty for playing out of turn in match play?

a) You automatically lose the hole
b) If you play out of turn, your opponent may cancel that stroke and make you play again

14 In tournament play, what should happen to golfers who break the guidance time (providing they're not being held up by the group in front)? The LPGA are certainly taking notice. A slow play penalty was issued at the 2023 Evian Championship and because Carlota Ciganda (pictured left) refused to sign her card with the penalty added, she was disqualified.

a) If a tournament official is present they are informed after three occurrences of 'bad time' and the fourth time garners a one-stroke offence

b) If a tournament official is present they are informed after the first occurrence and the second time it happens a player is given a one-stroke penalty. The third time, it's a two-stroke penalty

15 A ball has rolled up against a rake in a bunker. Moving the rake will cause the ball to move, and you can't play it as it lies. What happens now?

a) Move the rake and play the ball from where it ends up

b) Move the rake and put the ball back where it was before. If it rolls, try again

16 Under the R&A and USGA's Rules of Golf guidance, 'a round of golf is meant to be played at a prompt pace.' What is the guidance time for playing a stroke?

a) 40 seconds
b) 50 seconds
c) 60 seconds

17 Providing you put an identifying mark on your ball, you can change your ball between holes – True or False?

18 If you accidentally hit your ball while taking a practice swing on the tee, does that count as your first stroke? Yes/No

19 On the green, what happens if you are doing a couple of practice putting swings and actually catch your ball and move it with the end of your putter? Do you have to...

a) Replace it and take a one stroke penalty
b) Play it from where it moves to with no penalty
c) Replace it from its original position with no penalty

20 Are you allowed to stand Out of Bounds to hit your ball that is in bounds, but close to the edge? Yes/No

HOLE 13
LE EURO GOLF

Golf has its own *lingua franca*, a common language understood by all. Even in France, despite the national obsession with *not* adopting English words into the vocabulary, when a golfer hits it to the side of the fairway they'll find their ball in *le rough*. And after finishing the round they'll end up in *le clubhouse*. However not all of the English has made it into common parlance on European golf courses. Try working out these terms from France, Italy and Spain.

1 What do they call a bunker in French?

a) *Le bunker*
b) *Le diable de sable*
c) *Le sable entrape*

2 If you were on an Italian golf course, what would you do with a *pallina*?

a) Try and cure it, it's a hook
b) Place it on a tee, it's a ball
c) Celebrate, it's a hole in one

3 In Spain, what are *hierros medios*?

a) Men's tees
b) Mid-irons
c) Holes with a fairway between two water hazards

4 When someone hits an errant tee shot on a French golf course, what is it good etiquette to shout (in a French accent)?

a) Attention!
b) Fore!
c) Balle!

5 On an Italian golf course – what would you do with a *zolla*?

a) Place it back on the fairway, it's a divot
b) Take it into a bunker, it's a sand wedge
c) Eat it, it's a well-known Italian chocolate snack bar

6 In a Spanish match play competition, what is the meaning of *empatados*?

a) It's a gimme
b) It means 'all square'
c) It means 'I concede the hole'

Las Colinas club, Alicante, Spain

7 In France, is it good to score a *oiselet*?

a) Yes, it's a birdie
b) No, it's a bogey
c) No, it's a double bogey

8 Most Italian golfers will take what off the tee of a par-4 or par-5?

a) *Legno*
b) *Bandiera*
c) *Spogliatoio*

9 When visiting a Spanish golf course, players should be aware of the *código de vestimenta*. What is it?

a) Dress code
b) Local rules
c) Teeing off times

10 In France, what is a *motte de gazon*?

a) A green
b) A tee
c) A divot

The golf course at Etretat in Normandy

HOLE 14
WATER HAZARDS

There are certain 'givens' in sport. Everybody loves to see a dog on a football pitch and in golf, every golfer loves to see their playing partner hit their ball into water. That's why playing golf is a great life lesson. A golfer has to learn to conceal their natural glee at the misfortune of others. Here are some of the world's most famous watery graves...

1 Wreaking havoc on the Augusta National course in Georgia is a watercourse that has ruined many a back nine score in the Masters. What is it called?

a) Tom's Creek
b) Rae's Creek
c) Jim's Creek

2 Jack Nicklaus described the opening hole of the Championship Course at Machrihanish, as the 'best opening hole in the world'. Players must drive across a sandy bay to find the first fairway, or play it safe and fall a long way short. If a golfer's ball ends up on the sandy foreshore what happens next?

a) If they can find it (free of seaweed), they can play it from where it lies
b) They have to take another tee shot. The Atlantic Ocean is out of bounds

3 Jean Van de Velde achieved golfing immortality in 1999 when he contrived to lose the Open Championship at Carnoustie. On the final hole, with the option of going for the flag (and showing panache) or laying up short, the Frenchman went for the flag, hit a grandstand, then ended up in which stream protecting the green?

a) Old Harry's Burn
b) The Brae Burn
c) The Barry Burn

4 Another fine final hole with a water hazard is the par-5 18th hole at Pebble Beach, which has the Pacific Ocean skirting the left-hand side of the fairway to the flag. This was a scene of a miraculous escape for Hale Irwin in 1984. Needing a birdie to force a play-off in the Bing Crosby Pro-am he hooked his drive towards the ocean (find it on YouTube), it bounced off a rock on the shoreline and ended up in the middle of the fairway – from where he made a birdie and then won the playoff. Competing in the 2000 US Open John Daly managed what score on this tricky hole?

a) 2
b) 10
c) 14

5 There is a substantial lake at the side of the 17th hole at Disney's PGA-rated Magnolia Course in Florida, which stretches from tee to green. What is the unusual attraction, (apart from a Mickey Mouse-shaped bunker)?

a) It has a series of dancing fountains illuminated at night, like the Bellagio casino resort in Las Vegas

b) Professionals are allowed to bring their fishing gear and try and catch the 10-lb bass stocked in the lake

c) The course hires out jet-skis once the last competitor is safely on the 18th hole

6 Many professional golfers love the Pete-Dye-designed Harbour Town Links in South Carolina. Like Pebble Beach, the final hole is fringed by the ocean to the left of the fairway. Where do golfers traditionally aim for the ideal line in to the pin?

a) At the red-and-white lighthouse at the harbour entrance
b) At the mizzen mast of the barque *Indigo*, part of the harbour's historic ships collection.
c) At the first green navigation buoy in Calibogue Sound

7 The par-three 17th hole at TPC Sawgrass in Florida, is one of the most famous island holes in golf, with a watery outcome for many/most of the amateurs that play it. How many golf balls are estimated to be lost there each year?

a) 20-30,000
b) 50-70,000
c) 100-120,000

8 At St Andrews the Swilken/Swilcan Burn crosses the 1st and 18th fairways. The famous watercourse has a unique feature. What is it?

a) It's protected by an Act of Parliament
b) It's the final stretch of the same burn used as the water source for the Glenfiddich whisky distillery upstream
c) It was where Mary Queen of Scots lost five 'featherie' golf balls in 1547

9 Wentworth was once the home of the Suntory Matchplay Championship and subsequently the BMW-sponsored PGA Championship event. To liven up the final hole, it was re-designed for 2010 with the stream that crossed the 18th re-channelled in front of the green to provide real jeopardy for those trying to make the green in two shots. The change wasn't widely welcomed, and, amusingly, in its debut tournament the professional who redesigned the hole found the water with his second shot. Who was it?

a) Ernie Els
b) Sergio Garcia
c) Colin Montgomerie

10 On which golf course would you find the Pow Burn?

a) Prestwick
b) Troon
c) Turnberry

HOLE 15
IRISH GOLFERS

Like the Scots, Irish golfers have a rich variety of traditional links courses to practice on, as well as some more recent gems, such as Tralee and Head of Kinsale. So when the wind blows they're not at all disadvantaged, and when it rains, well, it just feels like home.

1 By any yardstick Rory McIlroy is a golfing genius, a man who has represented both Northern Ireland and Ireland in competitions and won four majors. Beginning the 2024 season he had yet to win the Masters, though. In 2011 he started his final round at 12-under-par, four strokes ahead of four other challengers. What happened next?

a) He scored 75 and lost by a single stroke
b) He scored a 76 and lost in a playoff to Charl Schwartzel who hit a final round 66
c) He carded an 80 and tied for 15th place

2 Becoming a golf professional can be a risky business, but Padraig Harrington always knew he had a profession to fall back on if the golf didn't work out. What is it?

a) He's a certified public accountant
b) He's a qualified lawyer
c) He's a registered CORGI gas engineer

3 Eamonn Darcy was a stalwart member of the Ryder Cup team across the years and played in 1975, 1977, 1981 and 1987. In his final Ryder Cup singles match in 1987, he won on the last hole to secure the team's 13th point and an outright win for the team. Who did he beat?

a) Larry Mize
b) Scott Simpson
c) Ben Crenshaw

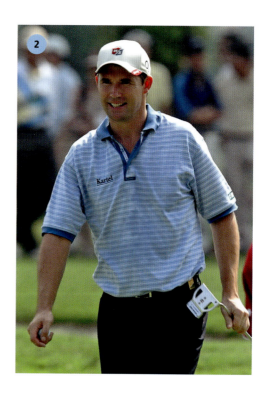

4 Which Northern Irish golfer became only the second European golfer in 85 years to win the US Open in 2010?

a) Darren Clarke
b) Graeme McDowell
c) Rory McIlroy

5 David Feherty was a pretty handy golfer in his time, winning five times on the European tour and playing in the 1991 Ryder Cup. He represented Ireland in international competition and captained the victorious 1990 Alfred Dunhill Cup team. Who were his team-mates?

a) Des Smyth and Ronan Rafferty
b) Philip Walton and Ronan Rafferty
c) Philip Walton and Des Smyth

6 Darren Clarke was the European hero of the 2006 Ryder Cup. He was one of Ian Woosnam's two wild card picks and earned three points on the way to victory for Europe in an event played at Ireland's K Club. What traumatic family event had Clarke suffered six weeks before the competition?

7 Dublin-born Padraig Harrington won his first major in 2007, the Open Championship at Carnoustie, after a four-hole playoff with which golfer?

a) Colin Montgomerie
b) Ernie Els
c) Sergio Garcia

8 Where did Shane Lowry win his first major title, the Open Championship, in 2019?

a) Royal Lytham and St Annes
b) Carnoustie
c) Royal Portrush

9 Normally winners of the Claret Jug get to keep it for a single year, but Lowry was allowed to hang on to it for two. Why?

10 Rory McIlroy and Shane Lowry are both supporters of which Premier League club?

a) Liverpool
b) Arsenal
c) Manchester United

11 Paul McGinley made Ryder Cup appearances in 2002, 2004 and 2006, with Europe being victorious each time. At the Belfry he secured the winning half point with a ten-foot putt and then jumped/was pushed by Sam Torrance into the lake – but which year?

a) 2002
b) 2004
c) 2006

12 Why would it be difficult for Padraig Harrington to sack his long-time caddy Ronan Flood?

a) Ronan is his accountant
b) Ronan is his godfather
c) Ronan is his brother-in-law

HOLE 16
THE US OPEN

The second 'major' to appear on the golf calendar, the courses chosen by the PGA represent a wide variety of challenges at which only the very best excel.

1 Rory McIlroy holds the record for the lowest total for four rounds – 268 – which he achieved at the Congressional Country Club in Bethesda in 2011. What was his score under par?

a) -12
b) -14
c) -16

2 Nice work if you can get it – the prize for the inaugural US Open in 1895 was $150 and a gold medallion (and presumably a round of stiff drinks). How much did Wyndham Clark take home for winning in 2023?

a) $2m
b) $2.75m
c) $3.6m

3 Who has started the most consecutive US Opens – a whopping total of 44 times?

a) Gene Sarazen
b) Gary Player
c) Jack Nicklaus

4 The second US Open was held at a course that is still used for the tournament today. Which venue played host?

a) Shinnecock Hills, New York
b) Winged Foot, New York
c) Pebble Beach, California

5 Jack Nicklaus won the first of his US Opens in 1962 in a playoff against Arnold Palmer. What was unusual about Nicklaus's win?

a) He played the third and fourth rounds to par with no birdies or bogeys
b) It was his first tournament win as a professional

6 England's Matt Fitzpatrick came home with a -6 score to win the event in 2022. On which course did he emulate fellow countryman Justin Rose?

a) Los Angeles Country Club, California
b) Pinehurst Resort, North Carolina
c) Brookline, Massachusetts

7 Which regular US Open venue is bisected by a two-lane turnpike?

a) Pinehurst, North Carolina
b) Brookline Country Club, Massachusetts
c) Oakmont, Pennsylvania

8 Four men have won the US Open four times – three are from the US; Bobby Jones, Ben Hogan and Jack Nicklaus. The final member of this quartet, Willie Anderson, is a tragic figure who won three in a row from 1903 to 1905 but died from epilepsy at age 31. What nationality was he?

a) Scottish
b) Canadian
c) Irish

9 The first US Open was held at the Newport Country Club, Rhode Island in 1895. When did the US get its first home-grown winner?

a) 1898
b) 1906
c) 1911

10 Which US state has hosted the most US Opens?

a) North Carolina
b) Massachusetts
c) Pennsylvania
d) New York

11 Who won the US Open in successive years (a rare feat) in 2017 and 2018?

a) Jordan Spieth
b) Brooks Koepka
c) Dustin Johnson

12 ...and who was the golfer that had last achieved this feat?

a) Arnold Palmer
b) Curtis Strange
c) Tiger Woods

13 Tiger Woods' first success at the US Open came in which year?

14 ....and what was his winning margin?

a) Seven strokes
b) Ten strokes
c) Fifteen strokes

15 Are female golfers allowed to enter the qualifying competitions for the US Open? Yes/No

16 US Open winners are invited back for how long after they lift the trophy?

a) The following year
b) Five years
c) Ten years

17 The record for the lowest score for 18 holes in the US Open was lowered to 62 in 2023 ... by two golfers! Rickie Fowler was the first – who was the second?

a) Wyndham Clark
b) Scottie Scheffler
c) Xander Schauffele

18 The US Open has been won wire-to-wire (leading all four rounds) by seven golfers. Who is the most recent?

a) Dustin Johnson
b) Martin Kaymer
c) Jon Rahm

19 US Open courses should have a range of qualities including undulating greens. But commenting on the 2005 event held at Pinehurst No.2 for NBC, Johnny Miller described the extreme undulations and pin placings as: 'like trying to hit a ball on top of ...' what?

a) The Houston Astrodome
b) A VW Beetle
c) Dolly Parton

20 The host venues for the US Opens to be held in 2049, 2050 and 2051 have already been chosen. True or False?

HOLE 17
GOLFERS' QUOTES

The best golfers are rarely short of something to say – unless of course they've had a terrible round and are heading for the car park. We have selected some golfing quotes that are famous and some that you can just imagine that particular player saying, all you have to do is match the quote to the player – they're listed at the bottom of the page. It's a dogleg question with the second part over the page

1 'I hit the ball as hard as I can. If I can find it, I hit it again.'

2 'Golf is the closest game to the game we call life. You get bad breaks from good shots; you get good breaks from bad shots – but you have to play the ball where it lies.'

3 'I played competitive golf all my life. Then all of a sudden, when I quit playing the game, I've got all this spare time and this energy. And certainly I wasn't ready to pack up my bags and go sit in front of the television with a shawl on.'

4 'Never beat yourself up. There are going to be plenty of people who are going to do that for you'

5 'There are far more important things in life than making a putt or missing a putt or winning a championship or losing a championship.'

6 'If you are caught on a golf course during a storm and are afraid of lightning, hold up a 1-iron. Not even God can hit a 1-iron.'

7 'If LIV Golf was the last place to play golf on earth I would retire. That's how I feel about it.'

8 'As my father taught me, and he drove home that point, he said, "Just remember something. You don't need to tell anybody how good you are. You show them how good you are." And he drove that home with me. So I learned early not to brag about how good I was or what I could do but let my game take that away and show them that I could play well enough.'

9 'I don't see a lot of guys that have done that (winning before the age of 24) besides Tiger Woods, of course, and, you know, the other legends of the game. It's just one of those things, I believe in myself and – especially with how hard I've worked – I'm one of the top five players in the world. I feel like I've proven myself.'

10 'I've travelled more than any human being who's ever lived.'

Gary Player	**Bobby Jones**
Tiger Woods	**Jack Nicklaus**
Bernhard Langer	**Rory McIlroy**
Lee Trevino	**Patrick Reed**
John Daly	**Arnold Palmer**

John Daly

Rory Mcilroy

Tiger Woods

Gary Player, Jack Nicklaus and Arnold Palmer

Bernhard Langer

Patrick Reed

11 'I'd like to see the fairways more narrow. Then everybody would have to play from the rough, not just me.'

12 'You only have one camera angle, that's all you can go off of, it's my word against their word. They weren't standing there.'

13 'Golf is a game of ego, but it is also a game of integrity: the most important thing is you do what is right when no one is looking.'

14 'I was more comfortable somehow in a European Tour setting. I have never really felt comfortable in the States and therefore I have never won a 72-hole event there.'

15 'I've always said golf can be a turn-off – all those middle-aged men in bad jumpers. I want to be a bit more of a character.'

16 'When I won the Dunlop Masters on the Burma Road course we played the four rounds in only two days. We certainly had to be fit. One thing is for sure. We did not spend time poncing about on the greens examining each putt, or studying yardage on the fairways. We did not have the time. We had to sum up the shot by eye and get on with it. The pace of play was far quicker and in my opinion this was no bad thing. Taking five hours or more over a round is ridiculous.'

17 'In twenty years' time no-one will remember what happened today.'

18 'They are scary ******** to get involved with. We know they killed Khashoggi and have a horrible record on human rights. They execute people over there for being gay. Knowing all of this, why would I even consider it?'

19 'Yeah, I'm definitely slower than average – have been my whole career. I definitely take my time. And when I hit my ball on a bulkhead, I'm definitely going to take my time to make sure I make the right decision and try to get the ball back into the right spot.'

20 'On 18 you've got to drive it up a gnat's ass.'

Ian Poulter	Tom Watson
Seve Ballesteros	Max Faulkner
Greg Norman	Patrick Cantlay
Colin Montgomerie	Phil Mickelson
Patrick Reed	Jean van de Velde

Phil Mickelson

Seve Ballesteros

Colin Montgomerie

Max Faulkner

Ian Poulter

Greg Norman

HOLE 18
NAME THAT GOLF COURSE – SCOTLAND

No country can offer the range of testing courses that Scotland has in abundance. And they're not all expensive. Golfers can play a round on historic, machair-lined fairways for a modest green fee. See if you can spot some of the better known courses, including those with precautions for wandering beasties...

ISLE OF BARRA
CASTLE STUART/CABOT
TURNBERRY
GLENEAGLES
LOCH LOMOND
LUNDIN LADIES

1

ISLE OF HARRIS
NORTH BERWICK
ST ANDREWS, OLD COURSE
ROYAL TROON
KINGSBARNS
CARNOUSTIE

HOLE 18 DOGLEG
NAME THAT GOLF COURSE – IRELAND

There are a variety of stunning golf courses in the Emerald Isle, from the K Club – scene of Ryder Cup action – to the dizzying cliff-top fairways of Head of Kinsale, to the Arnold Palmer-designed links at Tralee, close to where David Lean's epic movie *Ryan's Daughter* was filmed. See if you can put a number to a name...

CASTLE DROMOLAND

ROYAL COUNTY DOWN

THE K CLUB

HEAD OF KINSALE

ROYAL PORTRUSH

TRALEE GOLF CLUB

BALLYLIFFIN GOLF CLUB

LAHINCH GOLF CLUB

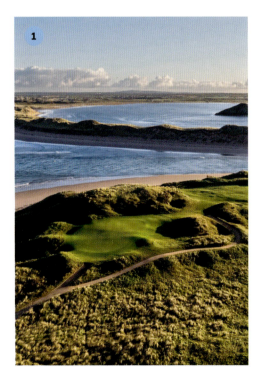

WEST COURSE:
THE FRONT NINE

1 UNUSUAL GOLFING HAZARDS
PAGES 92-95

2 THE RYDER CUP
PAGES 96-103

9 CHOKES AND BLUNDERS
PAGES 124-127

8 MAVERICKS
PAGES 120-123

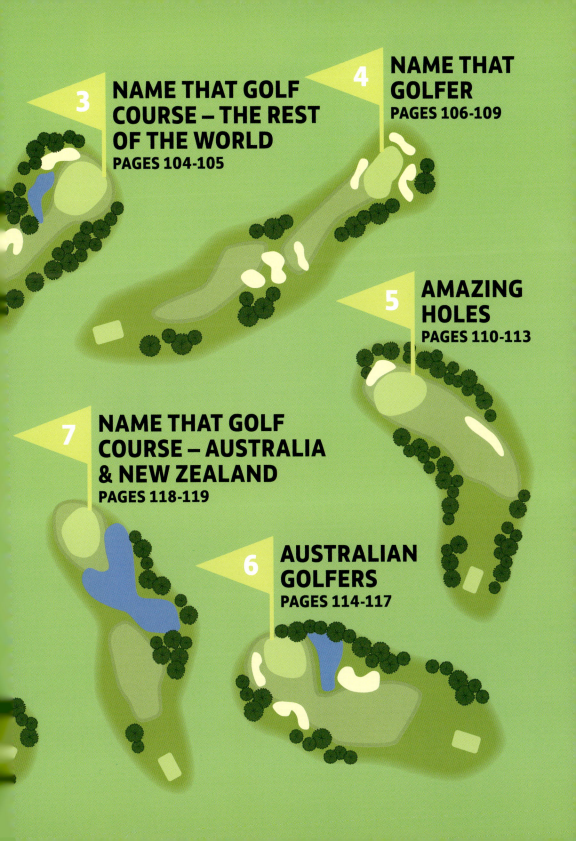

HOLE 1
UNUSUAL GOLFING HAZARDS

Apart from deep rough, water hazards and a wide array of bunkers there are other dangers that can be encountered on the world's golf courses. And quite often they live in the deep rough, water hazards and a wide array of bunkers... Plus there are the unexpected events – thunder and lightning and rogue golf carts

1 The Montana State Department of Fish and Wildlife advises golfers playing on the Gallatin, Helena, and Lewis and Clark National Forest golf courses to be aware of bears, especially if veering off into the rough stuff. They advise golfers to wear something to alert bears of their presence, but not to startle them unexpectedly. What did they suggest?

a) Fluorescent clothing, such as yellow, orange or lime green
b) Noise-producing devices such as little bells

2 Around 15,000 people a year are injured in golf buggy accidents, of which 10% are rollovers. Almost 6,500 of these injuries occur to which group of people?

a) Children and teenagers
b) Golfers under the influence of drugs or alcohol
c) Seniors

3 Death Valley is famous as the hottest place on earth and driest place in North America. The world's highest ever air temperature of 134°F (57°C) was recorded at Furnace Creek on July 10, 1913. So naturally there's a golf course at Furnace Creek. With just 1.6 inches of rainfall each year it relies on natural springs for its irrigation system. Apart from the intense heat, there's also the hazard that a coyote might pick your ball off the fairway. What do members jokingly call their annual competition?

a) The Heatstroke Open
b) The This-is-not-Scotland Open

4 Golf is often thought of as one of the most dangerous activities to be undertaking if there is a thunderstorm nearby. Statistically, who is most at risk?

a) Golfer
b) Fisherman
c) Farmer

5 Black bears often shy away from contact with humans. In case they don't respond to the precaution listed in Question 1, golfers are advised to carry what in their golf bags?

a) A powerful BB gun
b) A personal attack alarm
c) Pepper spray

6 At the Ness Golf Club, a nine-hole course just outside Reykjavik in Iceland, members are advised to take an umbrella with them if they go into the rough. They can be attacked by nesting seabirds which make a dive for the highest point of the golfer available. If that doesn't dissuade the player, they can also unload some guano in the golfer's direction. Which animal is responsible for this behaviour?

a) Puffin
b) Razorbill
c) Arctic tern

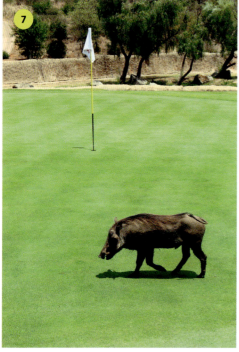

7 However, nothing can beat the variety of beasts at the Skukuza Golf Course in the Kruger National Park, South Africa. It has the entire cast of *The Lion King* wandering across its fairways. There are lions, hyenas, baboons, hippos, warthogs, hyenas, cheetahs and giraffe straying onto the unfenced nine-hole course. A lion once killed a buffalo on the first green. There is also a water hazard with crocodiles and an appropriate name. What is it?

a) Lake Hakuna Matata
b) Lake Panic
c) Lake of No Return

8 Carbrook Golf Club in Queensland has a unique threat to golfers in their water hazard, brought about when the local Logan River broke its banks and flooded the course and its large lake. What lurks in the water now?

a) Bull sharks
b) Box jellyfish
c) Piranhas

9 Australia is the home of many poisonous animals, but golfers at the Coast Golf and Recreation Club in Sydney have to be particularly aware, after one creature was found at the bottom of the cup on the second green. What was lurking below the flagstick?

a) A Sydney funnel-web spider *Atrax robustus*
b) A four-foot red-bellied black snake
c) A thorny devil lizard

10 They're not fearsome creatures, burrowing owls. But they can really make a mess of a golf course bunker. And golfers who hit shots into the burrows rarely get them back. Which tournament were they a feature of?

a) The 2023 Lofoten Islands Open
b) Olympic golf in Rio
c) Olympic golf in Japan

11 Mobs of kangaroos and wallabies populate many Australian golf courses with no trouble (apart from the obvious reminders left on the fairways), but at Riverside Oaks Golf Resort in Sydney they have started to take out the flagsticks and bury them in bunkers. True or False, Skip?

12 At Myakka Pines Golf Club in Englewood, Florida, members are quite familiar with alligators on the course. Mickie Zada, Myakka's general manager told the *Guardian* newspaper that the state wasn't a good place for herpetophobics (a fear of reptiles): 'It's impossible to play 18 holes and not see at least one alligator,' Zada said. 'When you're in Florida, you're going to see alligators.' What is the local rule if an alligator is on the green with your ball?

a) Count it as a two putts – but don't retrieve it, even if it's a Titleist Pro VIX
b) Count it as one putt – it's your lucky alligator day

HOLE 2
THE RYDER CUP

The biennial contest between Europe and the USA has produced truly memorable shots, nerve-shredding finales and wild celebrations over the years. Two years is just enough time to calm down afterwards, but how much of the events can you remember?

1 English businessman and golf enthusiast Samuel Ryder sponsored the first event in 1927. How did Ryder make his money?

a) Selling penny packets of seeds by mail order
b) Renting Model-T Fords
c) Importing the rubber used for the cores of golf balls

2 Who was the Great Britain and Ireland Ryder Cup captain who managed to score a rare victory at Lindrick, Yorkshire, in 1957?

a) John Jacobs
b) Dai Rees
c) Henry Cotton

3 Who is the youngest player to represent the European team?

a) Rory McIlroy
b) Sergio Garcia
c) José María Olazábal

4 The following players all made their Ryder Cup debut at 21? Who was the youngest of this trio?

a) Rickie Fowler
b) Jordan Spieth
c) Tiger Woods

5 Who is the oldest player to have taken part for either team at 51 years old?

a) Ray Floyd
b) Lee Westwood
c) Miguel Ángel Jiménez

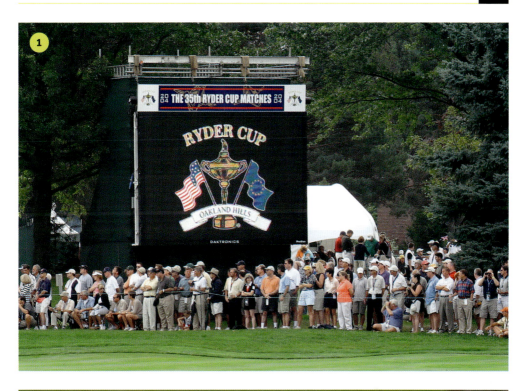

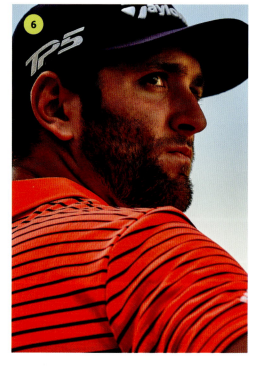

6 Who said: 'I'd love to play against Tiger. Scores are tied, Sunday singles, it'd be a dream to be able to compete against Tiger Woods for the Ryder Cup. That would be amazing ... unless I lose.'

a) Jon Rahm
b) Ian Poulter
c) Shane Lowry

7 In an act of great sportsmanship – for which he was criticized by his own team – which American player conceded a short birdie putt to halve a hole and a match against Tony Jacklin, saying to the British player: 'I don't think you would have missed it, but I wasn't going to give you the chance either.'

a) Lee Trevino
b) Jack Nicklaus
c) Tom Watson

8 The words 'legend' and 'legendary' are overused in sport, but one British Ryder Cup player deserves that tag. This golfer beat Jack Nicklaus twice in one day at Laurel Valley in the Ryder Cup. His legend grew when he admitted to Nicklaus afterwards that he was 'drunk as a monkey' in both matches. 'You never even knew he was having a drink. He was an alcoholic,' Nicklaus said in 2016. 'But he beat me twice.' Who was it?

a) Brian Barnes
b) Christy O'Connor Senior
c) Peter Alliss

9 Ian Poulter's nickname at the Ryder Cup has been 'The Postman' because he always delivers for the European team. Has he ever lost a Singles match in seven appearances – Yes/No

10 After a meeting between Jack Nicklaus and the Earl of Derby it was decided that something should be done to make the Ryder Cup more of a contest in the post-War period, which saw unprecedented dominance by the US team. When were European players first involved?

a) 1979
b) 1981
c) 1983

11 Veteran pro John Jacobs was the captain of the 1979 European team, which included two players who were troublesome right from the start of the tournament played at The Greenbrier, West Virginia. 'They behaved unbelievably stupidly,' said John Jacobs, 'From the word go when they appeared at the airport dressed as though they were going on a camping holiday.' One went on to become a Ryder Cup captain and the other a leading BBC golf commentator. Who are they?

12 Who's this playing out of a bunker for Team USA in 2004? Here's a clue, he was a contender in the 2023 Open Championship.

13 Which has been the most common pairing for the United States in the Ryder Cup?

a) Patrick Reed and Jordan Spieth
b) Tom Kite and Curtis Strange
c) Steve Stricker and Tiger Woods

14 Which has been the most common pairing for Europe in the Ryder Cup?

a) Luke Donald and Ian Poulter
b) Sergio Garcia & Lee Westwood
c) Seve Ballesteros & José María Olazábal

15 Following the arrival of European players in the team, the first host venue outside of Britain or Ireland was where?

a) Alcanada, Mallorca
b) Valderrama, Andalucia
c) Vale do Lobo, Portugal

16 In the 2023 Ryder Cup, the American team were criticized for being 'ring rusty' in their 16½-11½ defeat, but who played the most games and came back with a winning record?

a) Patrick Cantlay
b) Brian Harman
c) Max Homa

17 This the Great Britain and Ireland Ryder Cup team from which year?

a) 1967
b) 1971
c) 1975

18 This is the US Ryder Cup from which year?

a) 1981
b) 1983
c) 1985

19 Tiger Woods has a losing record in the Ryder Cup. True or False?

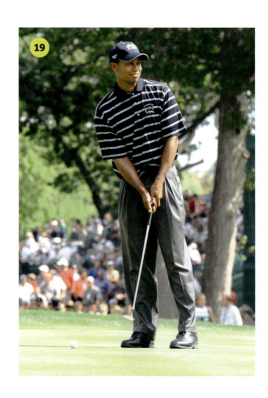

20 In 1999 at Brookline, which American golfer hit the 45-foot putt that saw the American team, including wives, invade the green before Europe had finished putting out?

a) Hal Sutton
b) JB Holmes
c) Justin Leonard

21 This is a photo of the starter's kiosk at Gleneagles. Which year did it host the Ryder Cup? The course, not the hut.

a) 2010
b) 2014
c) 2018

22 At the 44th Ryder Cup in Rome which European duo inflicted a record 9&7 defeat on Brooks Koepka and Scottie Scheffler in the Saturday Foursomes?

a) Hovland and Aberg
b) Aberg and Straka
c) Højgaard and Aberg

23 The Europeans were successful at the Marco Simone course in 2023, but why is only Viktor Hovland posing with the winning trophy and the European wives and girlfriends?

a) He was the first player to score a victory in the Sunday Singles
b) He was the player who scored the winning point for Europe in the Sunday Singles
c) He was the only single player for Europe

24 Who has won the most matches at the Ryder Cup – for either Europe or the United States?

a) Jack Nicklaus
b) Arnold Palmer
c) Ben Crenshaw
d) Sergio Garcia
e) Lee Westwood
f) Ian Poulter

25 When was the last time either Europe or the USA won 'away from home'?

a) Medinah Country Club, (Europe win)
b) Le Golf National, Paris (US win)

HOLE 3
NAME THAT GOLF COURSE
– THE REST OF THE WORLD

Golf is truly a world sport with courses on every continent except Antarctica. Here are some of the most spectacular courses from the rest of the world (that's barring the US, Canada, Australia, New Zealand, Europe, Scotland and Ireland, which have their own rounds). See if you can geolocate them...

BANGKOK GOLF RESORT, THAILAND

GLORIA GOLF CLUB, BELEK, ANTALYA, TURKEY

MEKNES GOLF CLUB, MOROCCO

KAU SAI CHAU GOLF CLUB, HONG KONG, CHINA

MERAPI GOLF CLUB, INDONESIA

FALDO COURSE, EMIRATES GOLF CLUB, DUBAI

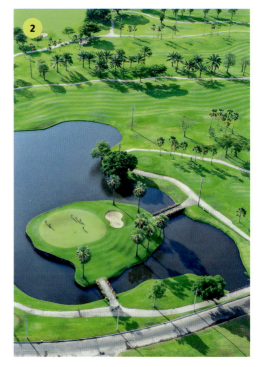

HOLE 4
NAME THAT GOLFER

We have assembled some of the greatest women golfers of today along with a few who have made an important impact on the game in the past. See if you can place a name to a number.

PAULA CREAMER

HYUNJU YOO

BROOKE HENDERSON

ATTHAYA THITIKUL

NELLY KORDA

MINJI LEE

GEORGIA HALL

INBEE PARK
MICHELLE WIE
BEATRIZ RECARI
LEXI THOMPSON
ANNIKA SÖRENSTAM
CELINE BOUTIER
LYDIA KO

HOLE 5
AMAZING HOLES

When Old Tom Morris was commissioned by the Royal North Devon club to redesign the Westward Ho! course (for the princely sum of £4) he thought that his giant fairway blocking bunker on the 4th hole might raise a few eyebrows. Some of the holes below have done the same in their time.

1 At Brocket Hall in Hertfordshire England, how do golfers reach the green on the 18th hole of the Melbourne Course?

a) By electric ferry
b) By a short cable car
c) By model railway

2 Following the popularity of island greens, more and more have appeared on modern golf courses. Despite having a reputation for slowing down play, Coeur d'Alene golf course in Idaho has one only reachable by boat – plus it's floating, so it can be anchored at a variety of distances off shore. This similar 'floater' par-3 seems a greater challenge (the photo is from the tee) where in the world would you find it?

a) Queenstown, New Zealand
b) Uttar Pradesh, India
c) Hunan province, China

Coeur d'Alene golf course, Idaho

3 Meadow Farms golf complex in Virginia, is the brainchild of Bill 'Farmer' Meadows. The multi-millionaire owner decided to go for novelty. And succeeded. Apart from an 841-yard hole, an island green, and a hole in the shape of a baseball ballpark, the par-3 4th hole of the nine-hole course is perched on top of a waterfall. True or False?

4 Although South Korea claims a 1,097-yard hole at the Gunsan Country Club, the official longest hole rests with Satsuki Golf Club in Japan. Their Hole 7 measures 964 yards. What par is it?

a) Seven
b) Eight
c) Nine

5 The Himalaya Golf Course in Pokhara in Nepal, is bisected by the fast-flowing Bijayapur River. What is the course's main claim to fame?

a) All the caddies are former Mount Everest sherpas
b) It has a river island green, with the river flowing either side
c) It is the highest golf course in the world

6 Respected golf designer Pete Dye, often assisted by wife Alice, is responsible for some of the world's most remarkable golf courses. These include the Brickyard Crossing Course in the US. The full 18 holes aren't playable throughout the year, as they're in the middle of the Indianapolis Motor Speedway. True or False?

The 4th tee is below the tree on the left

7 At Painswick Golf Club in Gloucestershire, on the par-3 4th hole named 'Castle', players have to lob tee shots up the hill to a blind green. The reason it's blind is that it is located at the top of a historic defensive fortification. Who built this great earthwork?

a) Ancient Britons
b) Romans
c) Saxons

8 The Llanmynech Golf Course – where Ian Woosnam learned his trade – is unusual in that it straddles the border between Wales and England. The fourth hole has a tee in Wales and a green in England. The fifth and sixth holes are wholly in England before the 'Welcome to Wales' sign appears before the seventh tee, with the rest of the course firmly in Wales. Why did this prove a particular problem during the Covid pandemic?

9 At Lundin Ladies Golf Club in Fife, Scotland, there is an unusual fairway hazard that golfers must avoid. What is it?

a) Bronze-Age standing stones
b) A Pictish burial chamber (golfers can claim relief if their ball lands on it)
c) The Glenrothes to Anstruther narrow gauge railway

10 At the Signature Course of the Legend Golf & Safari Resort in South Africa, there are eighteen holes each designed by a top golfer. Trevor Immelman designed the first, Bernhard Langer the 4th, Colin Montgomerie the 6th etc. However, all their fine work is trumped by the 'Extreme 19th' which has an enormous green in the shape of Africa and a tee perched high on Hanglip Mountain. To get there players need to take a helicopter ride to play the 690-yard hole. It's still a par-3, but what is the drop between tee and green?

a) 245 yards
b) 400 yards
c) 1,050 yards

HOLE 6
AUSTRALIAN GOLFERS

Punching well above their weight for star players, Australia has produced a number of major winners and in terms of the Official Golf World Rankings, the position of GOAT Junior. And it's not just the male players that are carrying the flag for the green and the gold, women players are at the top of their game too. See how well you know these stars from Down Under...

1 Rory McIlroy's engagement to tennis star Caroline Wozniacki didn't work out, neither did Adam Scott's relationship with Anna Ivanovic, but Greg Norman was married to which tennis star?

a) Martina Navratilova
b) Sue Barker
c) Chris Evert

2 Min Woo Lee announced his arrival on the European tour with a win at the Scottish Open in 2021, beating Matt Fitzpatrick and Thomas Detry in a playoff. Previous winners have included Rory McIlroy, Xander Schauffele, Phil Mickelson, Justin Rose, Rickie Fowler and Martin Kaymer. What is his best finish in a major – a tie for 5th place?

a) US Open 2023
b) Open Championship 2023
c) Masters 2022

3 It's slightly ironic that Adam 'Scotty' Scott, is also known as 'The Big Queenslander' as he was born in Adelaide, South Australia. How tall is he, though?

a) 6' (183cms)
b) 6'2"(188cms)
c) 6'5"(195cms)

4 Jason Day is another 'big Queenslander' who attended the golf academy at Hills International College, Jimboomba, when he was a teenager. While he was there he borrowed a book about which sportsman that inspired him to practice in every spare moment ?

a) Gary Player
b) Cricketer Dennis Lillee
c) Tiger Woods

5 In March 2022, Cameron Smith won The Players Championship at TPC Sawgrass, becoming the fifth Australian to win the tournament, despite hitting his second shot on the final hole into the water. But which Aussie golfer had won it twice before?

a) Stuart Appleby
b) Steve Elkington
c) Ian Baker-Finch

6

6 What does Min Woo Lee have in common with F1's Daniel Ricciardo, Tour de France cyclist Jai Hindley, cricketer Adam Gilchrist and tennis player Margaret Court?

a) They are all Western Australians
b) They are all Queenslanders
c) They are all sports stars who have sustained a bite from a redback spider

7 Min Woo Lee's older sister is a successful professional too, in the world's top 50. It is...

a) So Mi Lee
b) Andrea Lee
c) Minjee Lee

8 Yet another Queenslander – though not so big – Cameron Smith skipped the conventional US college route into professional golf and turned pro when he was 20. His record at the Masters is very good and in seven visits he has never missed the cut. True or False?

9 Wane Grady is well-known to BBC viewers for his commentary at the Open, a tournament where he was runner-up back in 1989. However, he won the PGA Championship at Shoal Creek in 1990, fending off which (now) veteran US player?

a) Chip Beck
b) Fred Couples
c) Loren Roberts

10 Steve Elkington's career has been hampered by battles with allergies, and one that is particularly cruel given his chosen occupation. What is it?

a) He's allergic to sand
b) He's allergic to grass and grass pollen
c) He's allergic to tree pollen

11 Which Australian golfer has won the most majors?

a) Greg Norman
b) Adam Scott
c) Jason Day
d) Peter Thomson

12 Peter Thomson was the consummate master of links golf. Between 1952 and 1958 his worst finishing position in the Open Championship was second place. He finished in the top ten of the Open an amazing 18 times. His profile in golf tends to be lower because he played very little on the US tour, yet he finished fifth at the Masters in 1957 and fourth at the US Open in 1956. How many times did he win the New Zealand Open?

a) Five times
b) Seven times
c) Nine times

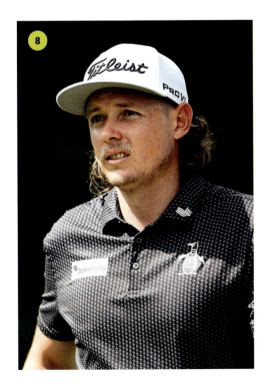

HOLE 7
NAME THAT GOLF COURSE – AUSTRALIA & NEW ZEALAND

Australia and New Zealand have produced some magnificent golfers, both male and female. They also have some of the most spectacular backdrops to their golf courses over a range of latitudes, from the sub-tropical to the distinctly nippy climate of New Zealand's South Island. See if you can place a name against these antipodean numbers, which include a venue that has native quokkas on the course...

BARNBOUGLE DUNES, TASMANIA

CAPE KIDNAPPERS, NORTH ISLAND, NEW ZEALAND

CAPE WICKHAM GOLD LINKS, KING ISLAND, AUSTRALIA

JACK'S POINT, QUEENSTOWN, NEW ZEALAND

QUEENSTOWN GOLF CLUB, KELVIN HEIGHTS, NEW ZEALAND

ROTORUA GOLF CLUB, NEW ZEALAND

ROTTNEST ISLAND GOLF CLUB, PERTH, AUSTRALIA

ROYAL MELBOURNE GOLF CLUB, AUSTRALIA

HOLE 8
MAVERICKS

There are the master shot-makers in golf that pull in the crowds, and also there are the entertainers. They are the players who are happy to stand out from the rest of their fellow professionals, or challenge the authorities, or play the game with such spirit that they are compulsive viewing whether they're winning or losing.

1 Ian Poulter is well known for his often 'outlandish' dress sense in the world of conservative golfing attire. He was once warned for wearing an Arsenal shirt during the Abu Dhabi Championship. In the 2005 and 2006 Open Championship he wore a pair of trousers imprinted with the famous Claret Jug. True or False?

2 Not that he has particularly big feet, but Swedish golfer Jesper Bo Parnevik was once described by golf writer Dan Jenkins as 'the last guy to climb out of the clown car at the circus'. The Parnevik look was a baseball cap with the peak upturned. To make him feel at ease when he played on the European team at the Ryder Cup, he received the standard team cap, but with the logo on the bottom of the peak, so it could be seen when he turned it up. True or False?

3 This Yorkshire golfer was known as a character, once marking his ball with a beer can and often smoking a pipe during his rounds : 'We're bloody entertainers,' was his response to those who questioned his antics. At the 1968 French Open he performed one of the biggest single-hole suicides in professional history. Falling short with a par putt and then lipping out the next, making it a bogey, he pulled the ball back for another go like it was match play, except it was stroke play. All tolled it came to a 15. Who was it?

a) Tommy Horton
b) Howard Clark
c) Brian Barnes

4 Payne Stewart's death in a Learjet that failed to pressurize, en route to a tournament in Houston, shocked the golfing world. Like Seve he was a man respected and loved and who upheld the values of the game. His regular donning of plus-twos and plus-fours on the golf course, along with old-school courtesy, reflected his passion for the traditions of golf. In which year did the sport lose one of the greats?

a) 1999
b) 2001
c) 2003

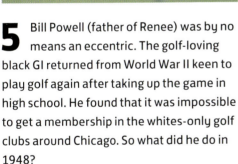

5 Bill Powell (father of Renee) was by no means an eccentric. The golf-loving black GI returned from World War II keen to play golf again after taking up the game in high school. He found that it was impossible to get a membership in the whites-only golf clubs around Chicago. So what did he do in 1948?

a) He enlisted the support of Dwight Eisenhower and joined the Congressional Country Club near Washington DC
b) He built his own nine-hole course and enlarged it to eighteen holes in 1978
c) He embarked on a cross-country, inter-state golfing expedition to raise awareness of the issue

6 Which US golfer, whose irons and wedges have shafts all the same length, is most linked with the Trump golf organization? In a 2020 interview he said: "I am extremely honored to represent Trump Golf and have the relationship with the Trump Organization that I have. From Larry Glick, to Eric Trump and Donald Trump Jr., the entire team is always behind me 100%, and I am grateful for their support.'

a) Pat Perez
b) Brooks Koepka
c) Bryson deChambeau

7 In 1999, who said: 'It's serious and we are both out here to win, but at the end I will shake Ben [Crenshaw] warmly by the throat and we'll have a beer.'

a) Tony Jacklin
b) Sandy Lyle
c) Mark James

8 In 1997 John Daly became the first PGA Tour player to average more than 300 yards per drive over a full season. He also has the rare distinction of being the only player to win two major championships and fail to be selected for the US Ryder Cup team. What's the highest placing that the Loudmouth Golf Apparel-sponsored player has achieved at the Masters?

a) Third
b) Twenty-third
c) He has never made the third round

9 American golfer Tom Kite said of Severiano Ballesteros: 'When he gets going, it's almost as if Seve is driving a Ferrari and the rest of us are in Chevrolets'. One of four brothers who all became golfing professionals, his older brother Manuel played on the European Tour for a decade. But it was his maternal uncle, Ramón Sota, who finished 6th in the 1965 Masters, a tournament that Seve won in which year?

a) 1980
b) 1982
c) 1984

10 It's not a haircut that's been widely adopted across the golfing world, Cameron Smith's mullet has been around since 2021. Representing Australia in the year-delayed Olympic Games he was able to shave the letters AUS into the side, just in case there was doubt in who he was representing. He first started nurturing his mullet during Covid-19 quarantine, but where did he get the idea?

a) Seeing John Daly videos on YouTube
b) From watching Aussie rugby league players with mullets
c) As a bet with his girlfriend that he could actually play a tournament with one

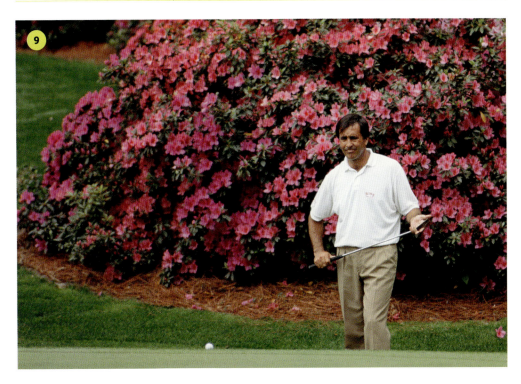

HOLE 9
CHOKES AND BLUNDERS

For those golfers who have duffed their opening tee shot simply because an elderly fourball have arrived on the first tee, the prospect of playing professional golf in front of paying spectators seems an impossible challenge. So when the pressure is on during prestigious tournaments and the professionals finally slip up, the hopeless amateur in all of us says a quiet 'yes', they are human after all.

1 One of the greatest chokes of all time was at the 1996 Masters where Greg Norman took a six-shot lead into the final round where he was partnered by Nick Faldo. Faldo shot a 67 – what did Norman finish with?

a) 73 – and he lost the subsequent playoff
b) 75 – he lost to Faldo by two strokes
c) 78 – he lost by five strokes

2 In 1986 Greg Norman held the lead after three rounds of all four majors (sometimes known as a 'Saturday Slam') a tremendous achievement in itself. How many victories did he pull off?

a) Three
b) Two
c) One

3 Scott Hoch rhymes with choke, which is what happened on the final green of the 1987 PGA Championship where he three-putted from inside ten feet, when two putts would have earned him a spot in the playoff. However, nothing compares with the two-foot putt that he missed on the 18th at the 1989 Masters (the putt he made back was longer) that sent him into a playoff with which European player?

a) Nick Faldo
b) Ian Woosnam
c) Sandy Lyle

4 'What a stupid I am...' Blunders don't just come on the course. Roberto de Vicenzo finished his final round at Augusta in 1968 believing he had made it into a playoff on -11. Unfortunately, though his score was indeed -11, playing partner Tommy Aaron had written down a four for the 17th hole, not the birdie three he'd got, and de Vicenzo signed the card without checking. So, officially he got a four and was -10. At which point the Argentine gave his famous quote. Who was the beneficiary of Tommy Aaron's adding up?

a) Billy Casper
b) Frank Beard
c) Bob Goalby

5 Not a choke, but a definite blunder. In the 1983 Open Championship at Birkdale, Hale Irwin went to tap in a birdie putt that came up inches short of the 14th hole cup. He went to tap it in casually for his par, his club hit the ground and passed over the ball, missing it entirely. There was the 'intent' to hit it and so that turned it into a bogey. 'I didn't bite myself,' Irwin said. 'But I kicked myself real hard.' Still on his mind, he went on to bogey the next hole, the relatively easy par-5 15th. Did it matter, though?

a) No, Tom Watson won the tournament by three strokes from Irwin
b) Yes, Tom Watson won by a single stroke from Irwin

6

Much is made of Jean van de Velde's final hole at Carnoustie where all he needed on the 18th was a double bogey six to become champion. The Frenchman hit a perfect drive, just ten yards short of the burn that winds across the final hole. A few minutes later he was contemplating his fourth shot from the same burn just in front of the green after a hack out of the rough had left him there. What added to Jean's indecision – and is generally underappreciated – is that the tide at Carnoustie was coming in, backing up the burn, and when he first looked at his watery lie, some of the ball was above the surface of the water. When he finally got in a position to play it, it was totally submerged. True or False?

7

Until Scott Hoch outdid him, Doug Sanders' closing hole of the 1970 Open at St Andrews was the classic 'biggest miss of all time'. Sanders had driven to within a short pitch of the green, virtually assuring him a par that would have won the championship. But his chip was poor and the recovery putt ended up three feet short... In later years Sanders joked that he didn't think about 'that putt' all the time. 'In fact, sometimes four or five minutes go by without me thinking about it at all.' Who beat him in the following day's 18-hole playoff?

a) Gary Player
b) Jack Nicklaus
c) Lee Trevino

8 How often do hotels ruin a golfer's tournament? In 2010 a major-winning player on the European tour circuit scorched round The Belfry in 64 strokes to lead by five after three rounds of the Benson and Hedges International Open. The Belfry Hotel asked if they could use some of the first round scorecards for a display in the foyer, which the organizers duly gave them. Some eagle-eyed staff member noticed that this player had not signed his first round scorecard – one of the other players in his group had signed it for him, contravening rule 6-6b. The leader of the competition was then disqualified half an hour before he took to the first tee. Who was it?

a) Padraig Harrington
b) Sergio Garcia
c) Sandy Lyle

9 The 2006 US Open at Winged Foot had players queueing up to lose it on the final hole. Phil Mickelson took a one-shot lead onto the 18th, hit a hospitality tent with a wayward drive, then hit a tree and made double bogey. Colin Montgomerie needed a par to win, a bogey to force a play-off, but unlike Mickelson hit the fairway with his perfect drive. And then missed the green with his second shot. A fifteen-minute wait for Vijay Singh to get a drop couldn't have helped – he came up short in the rough and eventually made a double bogey. Who won?

a) Geoff Ogilvy
b) Jim Furyk
c) Steve Stricker

10 Thomas Bjørn and sand were not great friends at the 2003 Open played at Royal St George's. Playing the 17th in the first round the Dane took an angry swipe at the sand which cost him a two-shot penalty and gave him a quadruple bogey. He recovered magnificently and led rookie Ben Curtis by three strokes with four holes to play. He bogeyed the 15th and then disaster struck on the par-3 16th when Bjørn put his tee shot into a deep greenside bunker. What happened next?

a) He blasted out and his ball went Out of Bounds
b) He blasted out and went into a bunker on the other side of the green, then three-putted
c) He needed three attempts to get out and then bogeyed 17

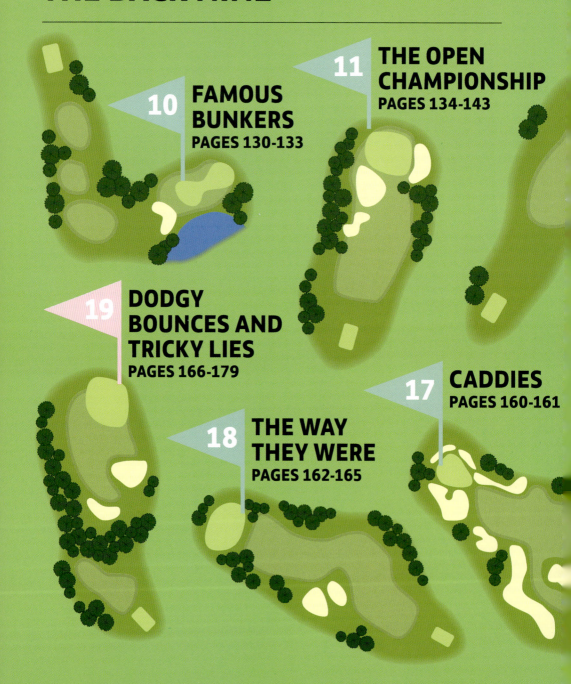

WEST COURSE:
THE BACK NINE

10 FAMOUS BUNKERS
PAGES 130-133

11 THE OPEN CHAMPIONSHIP
PAGES 134-143

19 DODGY BOUNCES AND TRICKY LIES
PAGES 166-179

18 THE WAY THEY WERE
PAGES 162-165

17 CADDIES
PAGES 160-161

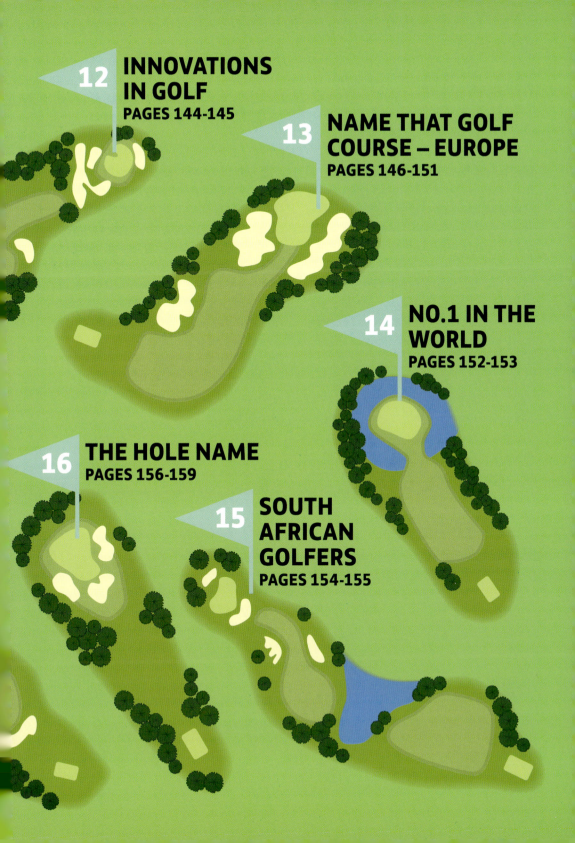

HOLE 10
WORLD FAMOUS BUNKERS

Sandy Balls is an area in England's New Forest which dates back to the reign of Henry VII and named after sand outcrops found in the heathland there. Today, golfers have to contend with more and more sandy balls than ever before as bunkers and sand traps proliferate on new courses, often a work of land art in their own right. Yes, we have reached the age of the theme bunker. See if you can answer questions on these corkers...

1 This pair of large bunkers that mirror each other, 64 yards short of the green on the par-5 14th hole at Carnoustie prevent anyone trying a traditional chip and run up to the flag. They have to be flown. Their name is the name of the hole. What are they called?

a) Spectacles
b) The Devil's Nostrils
c) The Twins

2 The long 14th hole on the Old Course at St Andrews features one of the world's best-known golf hazards, part of the reason that it is stroke index 1 on the scorecard. This sprawling bunker covers an area of some 300 square yards and in 1995 Jack Nicklaus took four attempts to get out of it, finishing up with a ten. Gene Sarazen tangled with it in 1933 and carded an eight, in a year when he missed a Championship playoff by a single stroke. What is it called?

a) Hades Bunker
b) Hell Bunker
c) Heart Attack Bunker

3 When he wasn't sprinkling bunkers on the Michigan shoreline, Pete Dye was creating huge single bunkers of almost geological proportion (and named accordingly). Alongside the 16th hole at The Stadium Course, PGA West, in La Quinta, California, there is a 20-foot drop to a long sandy ribbon. Put your ball in there and the raking will probably be worse than getting your ball out of it. What is this monster called?

a) The Mariana Trench
b) East African Rift Valley
c) The San Andreas Fault

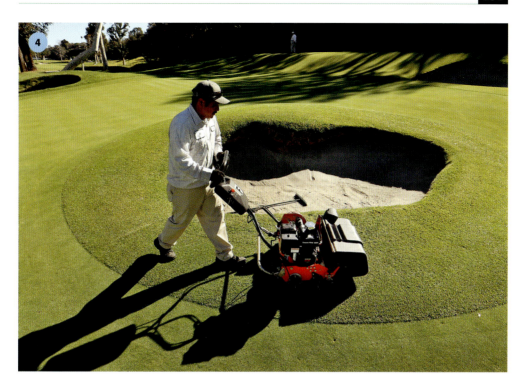

4 The 6th hole at the Riviera Country Club in California has a rare feature, especially for a tournament course. It has a small bunker in the middle of the green. The 199-yard par-3 hole can see golfers (one time including an exasperated Phil Mickelson) land their tee shot with the bunker between ball and pin. If that were to happen, would they be allowed to take a chip shot from the putting green? Yes/No.

5 This recent course truly embraces the concept of the sprawling bunker. Where would you find this beautiful 15th hole?

a) Cypress Point, California
b) Chambers Bay, Washington State
c) Kiawah Island, South Carolina

6 In May 2010 *Golf Digest*'s Ron Whitten and Bob Palm made a count of the bunkers at Whistling Straits and came up with a total of 967. They found the 8th hole had the most bunkers, 102, (almost as many as the whole of St Andrews) followed by the 18th, which had 96. What is strange about the world's most sand-trap infested golf course, though, is that it's built on clay, unlike natural links courses where sand comes free of charge. How many truckloads of sand did Pete Dye need to paint his masterpiece?

a) 2,000
b) 7,000
c) 13,000

7 The Harborside International Golf Center has a challenging par-3 15th hole. As part of the challenge it has a unique anchor-shaped bunker, one that is far better appreciated by a golf ball heading towards the green than a golfer at ground level. Where would you find this proper nautical curiosity?

a) Chicago, Illinois
b) Savannah, Georgia

8 These bunkers are a familiar sight lining the fairway between the third and fourth holes at the challenging Oakmont course. They used to be six separate bunkers, but for the 1935 US Open they were amalgamated into one giant bunker with six berms. In 1973 they got an extra two berms, and then in 2005 they got an extra four, making it the twelve we see today. What is the bunker called?

a) The Church Pews
b) Adam's Ribs
c) The Apostles

9 The Road Hole bunker is an old school pot bunker guarding the 17th green at St Andrews and it has been the undoing of many final rounds. What is the extra layer of jeopardy that golfers have to avoid on the opposite side of the green?

a) An Out of Bounds
b) The Swilken/Swilcan Burn
c) An even deeper pot bunker known as 'Old Tom's Undoing'

10 A towering bunker on the dogleg fourth hole at Royal St George's shares the same name as a similarly profiled bunker on the St Enodoc Course in Cornwall – they are both called...

a) Ben Nevis
b) Himalaya
c) Mountain

11 England's oldest golf links, the Royal North Devon at Westward Ho! has many hazards including sheep and horses that graze the course and coastal erosion which is making inroads into the playing area. And on the 4th hole there is a massive fairway obstruction lined with railway sleepers below which is an ocean of sand. What is it called?

a) The Cape Bunker
b) The Big Sandy
c) The Warren

12 The Coffin Bunker (one of a few bunkers called The Coffin, actually) is ready to nail errant tee-shots at a famous 8th hole on the Ayrshire coast. In the 2016 Open Championship Bubba Watson had played the first seven holes in five under par, but made a triple-bogey six on this 123-yard par-3, after drilling into The Coffin next to the green. Eventually Bubba conceded that he had to play out backwards to get anywhere. 'That hole has been killing me all week, even in practice' he said afterwards. What is the name of this famous hole?

HOLE 11
THE OPEN CHAMPIONSHIP

Golf's oldest international competition was only contested by a handful of players in the early years. Once the Royal and Ancient provided enough prize money to make a transatlantic crossing worthwhile, it was able to attract the very best American professionals to what is now a truly global tournament.

1 After its founding, there was a Scottish winner of the event for how many years?

a) Twelve
b) Nineteen
c) Twenty-nine

2 Which former Open course now sits almost entirely within a racecourse and has been reduced to nine holes?

a) Wincanton
b) Musselburgh
c) Elie and Earlsferry

3 The famous claret jug trophy dates to 1873 – winners hold it for a year and then have to exchange it for a replica, but what was the original winner's reward?

a) A silver salver
b) A gold medal
c) A championship belt

4 Young Tom Morris is the youngest player to win the Open Championship at 17, a record that is unlikely to be beaten. Tom Watson would have become the oldest at 59 had he finished off his 72nd hole at the 2009 Open at Turnberry with a par, but was forced into a playoff when he carded a bogey. Who retains the title as oldest winner?

a) Stewart Cink
b) Peter Thomson
c) Old Tom Morris

5 The first Open in 1860 was a small field limited to professional golfers. How many did the organizers manage to assemble for the 'first major'?

a) Four
b) Eight
c) Fourteen

6 The 1999 Open at Carnoustie will always be remembered for Jean van de Velde's attempts to tame the 18th hole. He was forced into a three-way playoff with eventual winner Paul Lawrie and which other golfer?

a) Justin Leonard
b) Stuart Appleby
c) Steve Elkington

7 St Andrews has hosted the Open thirty times. Which is the most-visited English course on the rotation of Open venues?

a) Royal St George's
b) Royal Liverpool
c) Royal Birkdale

The par 3, 12th hole at Royal Birkdale

8 Many were surprised by Brian Harman's win at the 2023 Open, but the Georgia-born golfer was 26th in the World Rankings at the time. Where was Ben Curtis on the PGA ranking when he won in 2003?

a) 111
b) 206
c) 396

9 Tiger Woods took his second and third Opens in successive years, 2005 and 2006. Who made it successive wins in 2007 and 2008

a) Padraig Harrington
b) Ernie Els
c) Retief Goosen

10 Crane operator Maurice Flitcroft was the subject of the film *Phantom of the Open*, which recreated his attempts to enter the Open by taking part in a qualifying round. Not having played on a golf course, or in possession of a handicap certificate, he simply declared himself a professional. Equipped with a cheap set of mail order clubs and practicing on local playing fields he recorded a score of 121, 49 over par (another record unlikely to be beaten). What year was Maurice's record set?

a) 1971
b) 1976
c) 1981

Maurice Flitcroft (right) pursues Seve in front of a *Daily Mirror* lensman at the Open championship he didn't quite qualify for.

11 What caused the Turnberry club – which hosted the memorable 2009 Open eventually won by Stewart Cink – to be taken off the rotation of courses used to host the event.

a) Its refusal to admit women members
b) The hike in green fees – almost double those of St Andrews
c) The events in Washington DC, January 2021

12 Who holed a sixty-foot putt on the 18th green to force a playoff in the 1995 Open – subsequently won by John Daly.

a) Constantino Rocca
b) Angel Cabrera

13 The first twelve Open Championships were held at one Scottish course and it wasn't St Andrews. Which Ayrshire club holds that distinction?

a) Royal Troon
b) Turnberry
c) Prestwick
d) Troon Dundonald

14 Tiger Woods dominated the Open in 2000. What contributed to his dominant win by eight strokes (apart from second place David Duval taking four shots to get out of the Road Hole bunker in his final round)?

a) He didn't miss a single fairway
b) He didn't find a single bunker

11

Second place Thomas Bjørn shakes hands with the Tiger mom.

15

16

15 The Fitzpatrick brothers, Matt and Alex, found themselves in the same major when younger brother Alex qualified for his first Open Championship in 2023. Who finished highest, tying for seventeenth place?

16 Hale Irwin labelled Seve Ballesteros 'The Car Park Champion' in 1979 after a wild drive from the 16th tee ended up in a temporary car park – and Seve got a free drop. Over 72 holes how many fairways did Seve hit on his way to winning the event?

a) None
b) Nine
c) Sixteen

17 Who holds the record for the lowest aggregate score at the Open – achieved at Royal Troon in 2016 with a final round flourish of -8?

a) Tomas Bjørn
b) Viktor Hovland
c) Henrik Stenson

18 A win at the Open guarantees the winner entry to the competition for how many years?

a) 10
b) 20
c) Until the age of 60

Not a dry eye in the house. Arnie bids farewell to St Andrews in 1995.

19 The first four-hole-aggregate-score playoff took place in 1989 when Mark Calcavecchia took on Wayne Grady and the fast-finishing Greg Norman, who had just come in with a mighty -8 final round. Who won?

a) Wayne Grady
b) Marks Calcavecchia
c) Greg Norman

20 The Open Championship cannot be held at Loch Lomond, Gleneagles or Wentworth for what reason?

21 To even out the playing conditions likely to be faced by competitors, players are allotted one morning start time and one afternoon start time. True or False?

22 *The Times* of London reported that there was a growing number of 'hopeless competitors' entering the Open and so in 1898 the first 'cut' in a major was introduced. In those days it was played over two days, with a round in the morning and a round in the afternoon. After 36 holes those not within nineteen shots of the leading score were cut from the competition (with a proviso that at least thirty-two professionals were allowed through). Seventy-six golfers teed off at Prestwick on Wednesday 8th June, how many made it through to play on the final day, Thursday?

a) Forty-three
b) Fifty-two

23 The famous 'Duel in the Sun' took place at Turnberry in 1977 with playing partners Jack Nicklaus and Tom Watson scorching ten shots clear of the field and prompting Tom Watson to say, 'This is what it's all about, isn't it.' On a day when Sandy Lyle, competing as an amateur, finished on +15, the world's two best golfers of the day finished on -12 and -11. But who won?

24 Who holds the record for the most second place finishes at the Open?

a) Jack Nicklaus
b) Tiger Woods
c) Phil Mickelson

25 Born in Jersey, in the Channel Islands, Harry Vardon holds the record for the most wins at the Open in 1896, 1898, 1899, 1903, 1911 and 1914. But what is he most famous for?

You're Nicked. The Scottish constabulary escort Jack Nicklaus from the 18th green at St Andrews. One of his winning years.

HOLE 12
INNOVATIONS IN GOLF

The handicap system and the Stableford scoring system are two inventions that have helped amateurs enjoy their game. But what golfers love most of all is a new club that will give them an advantage...

1 Wooden golf clubs in the 17th and 18th century were made from which trees?

a) Ash and hazel
b) Willow
c) Hickory

2 Frank Thomas of the Shakespeare Sporting Goods Company conceived and created what golf innovation in 1969? It was introduced at the PGA Show in 1970, however, it did not catch on with the masses straight away. What was it?

a) The electric powered golf trolley
b) The first graphite-shafted club
c) The first perimeter-weighted putter

3 Seamless tubular shafts arrived in the 1920s and in 1924 the USGA allowed them to be used in the 1924 US Open... for one club only. Which was it?

a) A driver, most commonly used teeing off
b) A putter, the most commonly used club
c) A 5-iron, the most commonly used fairway iron

4 Until the end of the Victorian period golfers would tee their balls on mounds of sand, or lumps of dirt. Two Scostmen, William Bloxsom and Arthur Douglas received a British patent for a tee in 1889, but the closest thing to our modern tees first appeared in 1899, though the top was flat not concave. Who invented it?

a) A Harvard-educated dentist, Franklin Grant
b) The 15th Earl of Atholl, Archibald Stokes-Allen
c) Socialite Martha Vanderbilt

5 Whistling shafts? Golf club makers experimented with solid steel shafts from the 1890s, but the big problem was making them light enough to swing. The development of hollow steel shafts was still a long way off. In 1915 an American inventor, Allan Lard, thought he had solved the problem by drilling hundreds of small holes in the solid bar to reduce weight. When a golfer swung the club, air passing through the holes made a whistling sound, thus his clubs were known as 'whistlers'. True or False?

6 Which golfer is widely regarded as inventing the sand wedge in 1932?

a) Bobby Jones
b) Gene Sarazen
c) Henry Cotton

7 Despite the innovation in America, the Royal and Ancient in St Andrews dug their heels in and put their trust in hickory, banning steel-shafted clubs until 1929. What event is said to have helped change the R&A's minds?

a) A sizable donation from the US firm True Temper who had pioneered the tapered step-down shaft
b) Leading Scottish golfer George Duncan bought a set
c) The Prince of Wales (later Edward VIII) used a set at St Andrews in 1929 and the committee took note

8 At the 1991 PGA Merchandise Show, Callaway introduced an oversize stainless-steel driver. The club was the idea of the company's designer Dick Helmstetter. At 190 cubic centimetres, the driver was about 30 percent larger than most drivers at the time but still considerably smaller than they are today. What was the name of this breakthrough piece of kit?

a) Big Bertha
b) Boomer
c) Big Bob

9 Which company were responsible for introducing the cavity-back iron in the 1980s

a) Ping
b) Taylor Made
c) MacGregor

10 Finally, a question not about equipment, but an innovation that has helped golfers of every level to enjoy playing in competitions. This system of scoring allows golfers to stay in the game even after one or two bad holes in a round. The Stableford scoring system sped up play, too, because golfers who could no longer score a point on a hole picked up their ball and moved on. It was first used in 1932 and has proved successful ever since. Who invented it?

a) Frank Stableford
b) Ken Stable and Patrick Ford
c) Frank Griffith of the Stableford Golf and Country Club in Hampshire

Gene Sarazen and Bobby Jones

HOLE 13
NAME THAT GOLF COURSE – EUROPE

With the 2023 Ryder Cup hosted by the Marco Simone Golf Club near Rome – following visits to France and Spain – the quality of top European courses is rising year by year. See if you can identify this *mélange* of new and established golf venues.

GOLF DE BIARRITZ, FRANCE

BRAUTARHALT GOLF CLUB, ICELAND

GOLF CLUB DE CHAMONIX, FRANCE

DUNSTANBURGH CASTLE GOLF CLUB, ENGLAND

VALE DO LOBO GOLF CLUB, PORTUGAL

BUDERSAND SYLT, SCHLESWIG HOLSTEIN, GERMANY

GOLF DU TOUQUET, LE TOUQUET, FRANCE

ARCHI DE CLAUDIO GOLF CLUB, ROME, ITALY

GIMSOYSAND GOLF CLUB, LOFOTEN ISLANDS, NORWAY

HARLECH CASTLE GOLF CLUB, WALES

TENERIFE GOLF CLUB, CANARY ISLANDS

VALDERRAMA GOLF CLUB, SPAIN

STADIUM COURSE, BRO HOF SLOTT, SWEDEN

TRANRÜS GOLF COURSE, CORVARA (THE DOLOMITES) ITALY

CLUB DE GOLF ALCANADA, MALLORCA, SPAIN

CRANS-SUR-SIERRE, CRANS-MONTANA, SWITZERLAND

CRETE GOLF CLUB, GREECE

GOLF D'ETRETAT, NORMANDY, FRANCE

HOLE 14
NO. 1 IN THE WORLD

The very first No.1 in the world was Scottish professional Alan Robertson, who was so good, the only reason golfers organized the first Open Championship was to find out who was No.1 after he died. Fast forward to the twenty-first century and we have the Official Golf World Rankings to monitor things...

1 The Official Golf World Rankings, or OGWR, were launched in 1986. Since that time, how many players have reached that coveted No.1 status?

a) 16
b) 25
c) 34

2 Only three golfers have managed to stay No.1 for a calendar year. Who?

a) Nick Faldo, Greg Norman, Tiger Woods
b) Dustin Johnson, Greg Norman, Tiger Woods
c) John Rahm, Rory McIlroy, Tiger Woods

3 Which of these countries has not had a No.1 golfer?

a) Wales
b) Zimbabwe
c) Scotland
d) Fiji

4 Which golfer has the rare distinction of making it to No.1 for one week only – many players have one-week stints at No.1, drop to No.2, then jump back to No.1. This golfer was a one-time wonder on the World rankings.

a) Tom Lehman
b) Justin Rose
c) Paul Casey

3

5 Who was the first European golfer to make it to No.1?

a) Seve Ballesteros
b) Bernhard Langer
c) Nick Faldo

6 There's no question as to who is the GOAT of the OGWR, Eldrick Tont Woods, with 683 weeks at No.1 (another record that is unlikely to be broken) has more than double the next contender. Which is his longest unbroken spell of world domination?

a) 173 weeks – more than three years
b) 229 weeks – more than four years
c) 281 weeks – more than five years

7 When the Tiger was toppled, in October 2010, who was it that took his place?

a) Lee Westwood
b) Rory McIlroy
c) Martin Kaymer

8 If you compare the nationality of golfers at No.1, the United States are runaway winners with 973 total weeks for US golfers at No.1. Australia are next mostly thanks to Greg Norman, followed by England. But which of these two countries is 4th on the list?

a) Spain
b) Northern Ireland

9 The OGWR ranks professional golfers (and you can probably guess what the OWGWR does too). To what position does the professional organization rank golfers?

a) 1-750
b) 1-2000
c) 1-8000+

10 Only one South African golfer has made it to No.1, and that for a measly nine weeks. Who was it?

a) Louis Oosthuizen
b) Retief Goosen
c) Ernie Els

HOLE 15
SOUTH AFRICAN GOLFERS

It all started with Bobby 'Old Baggy Pants' Locke in 1947, when he hosted Sam Snead for a series of exhibition matches in South Africa and won twelve out of the sixteen. Snead suggested he come and play on the PGA tour and even though he didn't arrive till April of that year, finished second on the money list. South African golf never looked back...

1 Gangly South African Christo Lamprecht was the surprise leader after the opening round at the Open Championship at Hoylake in 2023. His 65 was the second lowest by an amateur in Open history. He went on make the cut and finished the tournament as leading amateur. How tall is he?

a) 6'5"
b) 6'8"
c) 7'

2 Gary Player is by far and away the most successful South African golfer, having won nine majors and designed 400 golf course in an extraordinarily full golfing lifetime. How many times did he play in the US Masters?

a) 26
b) 33
c) 52

3 Which South African golfer said: 'It's a marriage. If I had to choose between my wife and my putter, well, I'd miss her.'

4 As a fifteen-year-old, Retief Goosen was playing on Pietersberg Golf Course when he was hit by lightning, which blew him off his feet and melted his watch to his arm. His father took this as a sign from God that his son was going to have a great career. True or False?

5 Charl Schwarzel, the golfer that every commentator wants to add an 'es' to, has won a single major. What is it?

a) The Masters
b) The US Open
c) The Open Championship

6 1984 was a vintage year in the Junior World Championship with David Toms winning the 15–17 years age group and Tiger Woods winning the 9–10s (despite still being age 8). Which South African golfer beat runner-up Phil Mickelson in the 13-14 years ages group…?

a) Trevor Immelman
b) Retief Goosen
c) Ernie Els

7 South African golfer Luis Oosthuizen is a second cousin of English golfer and former broadcaster Peter Oosterhuis, whose family shortened their name when they moved to London from Johannesburg in the late 1940s. True or False?

8 Mission Hills in China is one of the world's largest golf facilities with ten courses each designed by a famous player. Ernie Els was responsible for one, joining a list of golfers that included Jack Nicklaus, Nick Faldo, Vijay Singh, Jumbo Ozaki, David Duval, coach David Leadbetter, José Maria Olazabal, Annika Sörenstam and Greg Norman. What is Ernie's course called?

a) Savannah
b) Pampas
c) Serengeti

9 Ernie isn't Ernie Els's given forename. Like Tiger woods, he has a more formal first name. What is it?

a) Theodore
b) Terence
c) Heinrich

10 Retief Goosen claimed his second US Open at Shinnecock Hills in 2004 on a day when the course won. A combination of heat and wind dried the ultra-fast greens out so much that greenskeepers were watering them in between groups. Goosen beat off the challenge of Phil Mickelson with a display of nerveless putting. None of the final rounds scores that day were below par. Fellow countryman Ernie Els carded an 80. What was the average final round score?

a) 74.8
b) 76.9
c) 78.7

HOLE 16
THE HOLE NAME

Many of the older golf courses have names attributed
to their holes – sometimes they even get re-christened
after events on the course. The par-3 'Postage Stamp'
hole was originally called 'Ailsa' because there was
a good view of Ailsa Craig island in the Firth of Clyde
from the tee. But writing in *Golf Illustrated* magazine
William Park wrote that the hole had: 'A pitching surface
skimmed down to the size of a postage stamp' and the
name stuck ... unlike many of the golf balls that have
landed on the green. See if you can match the list of hole
names to their respective courses.

DINARD, FRANCE

TRALEE, IRELAND

SPYGLASS HILL, UNITED STATES

AUGUSTA NATIONAL, UNITED STATES

OLD COURSE, ST ANDREWS, SCOTLAND

1 White Dogwood
Azalea
Magnolia
Firethorn
Camelia
Juniper

2 Bobby Jones
Cartgate
Corner of the Dyke
Heathery
Road Hole
Tom Morris

3 Treasure Island
Billy Bones
The Black Spot
Israel Hands
Admiral Benbow
Jim Hawkins

4 Mucklough
The Castle
The Randy
Brock's Hollow
Poulgorm
Ryan's Daughter

5 Le Tennis
La Garde
La Joie
La Plage
Les Baigneuses
La Terrasse

Augusta National, United States

Dinard, France

ROYAL LIVERPOOL, HOYLAKE, ENGLAND
CARNOUSTIE, SCOTLAND
SHINNECOCK HILLS, UNITED STATES
MACHRIHANISH, SCOTLAND
ROYAL TROON, SCOTLAND

6 Battery
Islay
Jura
Gigha
Punch Bowl
Balaclava

7 Seal
Black Rock
Dunure
Greenan
Rabbit
Postage Stamp

8 Telegraph
Briars
Dowie
Far
Dee
Alps

9 Westward Ho
Eastward Ho
Peconic
Montauk
Sebonac
Ben Nevis

10 Jockie's Burn
Gulley
Hogan's Alley
Brae
Barry Burn
Southward Ho

Shinnecock Hills, United States

Royal Liverpool, Hoylake

Royal Troon, Scotland

HOLE 17
CADDIES

They're an essential part of the professional tour – carrying a bag round is probably the easiest element of what can be a very demanding, multi-skilled job – everything from psychotherapy to club maintenance and crowd control. How much do you know about a player's right-hand man (or woman)?

1 What is the origin for the term caddy ?

a) It's from the Malaysian *catti* – a catti was the standard one-and-a-quarter-pound bag of tea, from which we get tea caddy, and hence a golf caddy held golf clubs
b) It's from the French cadet, or boy – who were the first caddies
c) The earliest boys helping out on St Andrews links were all from the local school, St Dunstan's Academy, which got shortened to a 'caddy boy'

2 Many of the top caddies earn in excess of $100,000 as a base salary. What percentage of the winner's prize money do they receive?

a) It's entirely discretionary
b) Generally ten per cent for a top-ten finish
c) Generally five per cent for a top-ten finish

3 The reason golfers shout 'fore!' to warn of a golf ball approaching is because early players on links courses needed a ballspotter up ahead. Anyone who's played on a links course will know that balls can take all kinds of awkward bounces into impenetrable rough and these 'forecaddies' were necessary to pinpoint exactly where expensive featherie balls had landed. Golfers would shout 'forecaddie!' to let them know the ball was on the way on blind holes. In time this has been shortened to 'fore!' as a general warning. True or False?

4 Matt Fitzpatrick won the US Amateur Open at Brookline in 2012 – and it was a family affair. Who was on the bag for Matt during the tournament?

a) Little bother Alex
b) Mum Sue
c) Uncle Ignacio

5 A caddie is not allowed to touch the sand in a bunker to advise a player of the condition of the sand. True or False?

6 It's not Formula 1, but this leading women's professional is spraying the champagne. But hang on, is it her caddie? Who's got the bottle...?

7 The Augusta National club insisted players use their Black caddies at the Masters until which year?

a) 1968
b) 1976
c) 1983

8 Swedish amateur golfer Fanny Sunesson has worked as a caddie for Henrik Stenson, Adam Scott, Sergio Garcia, Ian Poulter and is pictured here with Michelle Wie. Who is she best known to have caddied for, a spell of almost ten years?

9 A caddie can mark, pick up and clean a ball that is on the green – provided it belongs to their player . True or False?

10 Kiwi Steve Williams was on Tiger Woods' bag for his most successful years 1999–2011. He was a vigorous defender of his boss, once allegedly throwing a spectator's camera into a pond for taking a photo on Tiger's downswing. Which Aussie golfer did he accompany to major success?

a) Adam Scott
b) Jason Day
c) Cameron Smith

HOLE 18
THE WAY THEY WERE

Given the amount of exposure on television, it would be a fairly simple exercise to identify today's leading golfers. In the NFL and Formula 1 the sportsmen spend a lot of time concealed by helmets, whereas out on the course the camera homes in on a player's every agonized (or deadpan) expression. So we have gone back into the archives to find photos of the stars before they grew that full ocean-going beard, or the four-day stubble, or adopted a trademark mullet. See if you can match the numbers to the players listed below.

RICKIE FOWLER

BROOKS KOEPKA

JON RAHM

SCOTTIE SCHEFFLER

RORY MCILROY

DANIEL WILLETT

TYRRELL HATTON

VIKTOR HOVLAND

CAMERON SMITH

MATTHEW FITZPATRICK

PATRICK REED

DUSTIN JOHNSON

JORDAN SPIETH

IAN POULTER

BRIAN HARMAN

SHANE LOWRY

THE 19TH HOLE
DODGY BOUNCES AND TRICKY LIES

The final hole in any round represents a tough challenge (even though the 19th is technically the bar). Assembled here are some very tricky lies along with some scarcely believable truths. See if you can navigate your way through to the finish without hurling any clubs into the bushes.

1 Island greens are considered an important element in new Asian golf courses where betting culture is an important part of the golf experience. A leading golf architect explained that the ability of an island green to settle the outcome of a bet almost instantly is one reason why these types of holes are popular. (This one is at Payne's Valley, Missouri, a course designed by Tiger Woods). True or False?

2 Bobby Jones may have been an amateur, but he was happy to bet on his own abilities for cash. In 1930 he placed a bet with bookmakers at 50-1 that he could win all four majors of that year. The Amateur Championship at St Andrews in May, The Open Championship at Hoylake, in June, the US Open at Interlachen Country Club in July and the US Amateur at Merion Golf Club, Pennsylvania in September. He collected $60,000 when he did it. True or False?

3 In 1907 the US Open was hosted by a cricket club. True or False?

4 The devil is a popular nametag in the United States, especially when it comes to siting golf courses. He pops up in the names of a number of clubs, including five of the following sextet. Which one have we invented?

a) Devil's Thumb, Delta, Colorado
b) The Devil's Butt, Moab, Utah
c) Devils Knob Golf Course, Virginia
d) Devil's Ridge Golf Club, Oxford, Michigan
e) Devil's Head Resort, Merrimac, Wisconsin
f) The Golf Club at Devils Tower, Hulett, Wyoming

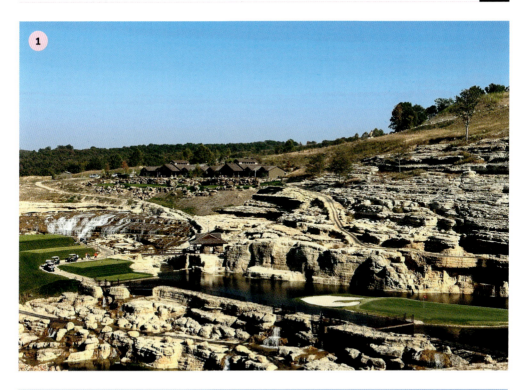

The Devils Golf Course is an area of barren rock in Death Valley, California

5 Which of these former golfers has not actually received a knighthood?

a) Sir Henry Cotton
b) Sir Bob Charles
c) Sir Tony Jacklin
d) Sir Nick Faldo

6 After his success as Supreme Commander of Allied forces in World War II, Dwight D. Eisenhower became a member of Augusta National. He became President in 1953 and had a cabin built on the grounds, with a basement set aside for Secret Service agents. During his time at the club he lobbied unsuccessfully to have what change made?

a) To admit Black members
b) To have an annual tournament for WWII and Korea veterans
c) To have the large loblolly pine on the 17th fairway removed

7 Republican presidents tend to spend more time on the golf course than Democratic presidents. In particular, Donald Trump has many golf interests and investments – what is his alleged handicap?

a) 2.8
b) 11.4
c) 17.6

8 Comparing handicaps, father and son (like Young Tom Morris and Old Tom Morris) George W. Bush was a better golfer than father, George H.W. Bush. True or False?

9 What do golfing celebs Celine Dion, Justin Timberlake and Clint Eastwood have in common?

a) They have all scored holes in one
b) They have all won pro-am tournaments
c) They all have multi-million dollar investments in golf courses

10 Astronaut Alan Shepard played the first extra-terrestrial golf shots when he took a Wilson Staff Dyna-Power 6-iron head (attached to a lunar rock sampling tool) and two balls to the moon on which Apollo mission?

a) Apollo 12
b) Apollo 14
c) Apollo 16

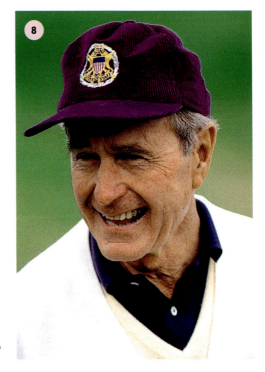

11 Shepard shanked his first shot, but his second, according to Alan, went 'miles and miles' in the low-gravity environment. Some years later, scientists were able to measure it from high definition photos and came up with what distance?

a) 534 yards
b) 266 yards
c) 40 yards

12 Which veteran golfer appears in the film, *Happy Gilmore*, but – when he saw some of the language used in the movie – wished he hadn't.

a) Lee Trevino
b) Jack Nicklaus
c) Tom Watson

Rory Mcilroy, Tiger Woods, Georgia Hall, Jack Nicklaus and Lee Trevino celebrating the 150th Open Championship at St Andrews.

13 What happened to the prize money paid out to the US winners in the Open Championship in 2017?

a) It was switched from £ to euros
b) It was switched from guineas to £
c) It was switched from £ to $
d) It was switched from $ to £

14 While at St Andrews University Kate Middleton did two important things. She met her future husband William Windsor and secured the job of future queen. More importantly she also discovered a great love of golf and was a regular player on the New Course where students at the university got discounted rates. True or False?

17 Jordan Spieth and Justin Thomas have invested in 49ers Enterprises the company looking to take the controlling financial interest in Leeds United Football Club. Rickie Fowler was going to invest too, but backed out when the club was relegated to the Championship in 2023. True or False?

18 Following the success of the Netflix F1 series *Drive to Survive*, the broadcaster has broadened out their sports documentaries to cover the Tour de France and professional golf. What is their golf series called?

a) *'Fore!'*
b) *Below Par*
c) *Full Swing*
d) *Birdie, Bogey, Par*

15 A Birdie is one under par, an Eagle is two under par, an Albatross three under par. What is the name for a hole that is played at four under par – i.e. a hole in one at a par-5, or two shots on the rare par-6 holes?

a) Hawk
b) Vulture
c) Condor

16 Which US golfer became a hero, (but sadly missed the cut), after helping deal with disruptive climate activists at the 2023 Open Championship?

a) Collin Morakawa
b) Billy Horschel
c) Tony Finau

19 Joyce Wethered, (pictured playing from sand at Fresh Meadows, NY, in 1935), won the British Ladies Amateur Championship four times in 1922, 1924, 1925 and 1929. Bobby Jones called her the best golfer, male or female, that he had ever seen. She suggested that a hole in one should be called what?

a) Curlew
b) Skua
c) Nightingale

20 We often read about bunkers and sand traps 'guarding' the fairway, but at Rye Golf Club in Sussex, England, what unusual military feature borders one of the fairways?

a) A World War II concrete pillbox
b) A World War I tank, preserved by the golf club after it was stranded there during trials in 1915
c) A British Army firing range

21 Iceland has the largest number of golf courses per capita in the world – and because of regular volcanic activity on the island there are local rules that apply. If lava encroaches onto the fairway that counts as any ordinary lateral hazard, however if a ball lands on volcanic ash that has fallen, a golfer is permitted to lift and place (as per winter rules). True or False?

22 Poet Laureate Sir John Betjeman, who wrote the classic poem *Seaside Golf,* is actually buried on a golf course in Cornwall. True or False?

23 During the 1949 Open Championship, Irish professional Harry Bradshaw hit a drive on the fifth hole of Royal St George's and the ball came to rest inside the bottom of a broken champagne bottle. Playing it where he found it, instead of asking for a drop, Bradshaw belted the bottle stump, glass splintered and the ball flew only a few yards, leading to a double bogey for the hole. True or False?

24 After his success at the 2023 Open Championship Brian Harman said he was looking forward to what…?

a) A night out with all his friends at the Bubba Gump Shrimp restaurant in Savannah, Georgia
b) A long-delayed blow-out weekend to Vegas to play Steve Wynn's golf course
c) Mowing the grass on his ranch with a new Kubota tractor

25 While many players on the PGA Tour attended US colleges on golf scholarships, Boo Weekley enrolled at the Abraham Baldwin Agricultural College in Tifton, Georgia. He retired from the Tour in 2018 and now breeds Rhode Island Red chickens on his farm near Willacoochee, Georgia. True or False?

22

26 There have always been a lot of Clarks (and Clarkes) in golf. Today, it's Wyndham who is the highest profile Clark after his US Open win. But let's not forget Howard, Tim, who won the Players Championship, and Darren Clarke who's an Open winner and a Senior Open winner. What nationalities are they?

a) American, English, Australian, Northern Irish
b) American, Australian, South African, Northern Irish
c) American, English, South African, Northern Irish

Greg and Tiger go way back. This is the duo practicing for the Masters in 1995 when Woods was an amateur.

27 Canterbury-based progressive rock band Caravan included the track 'Golf Girl' on their 1971 album, *In the Land of Grey and Pink*. What was the golf girl doing on the golf course?

a) Selling cups of tea
b) Embroidering smiley faces on the flags of flagsticks
c) Sunbathing by the 14th green

28 Colin Montgomerie and Ian Woosnam once appeared together in a TV advert that gently self-mocked Monty's sometimes irascible behaviour on the golf course, especially when disturbed by a spectator. What were they advertising?

a) Fosters – lager
b) Nurofen – pain relief
c) KitKat – chocolate wafer bar

29 LIV Golf reportedly offered Sergio Garcia $40 million to sign up to the Saudi-backed tour and he said yes. Tiger Woods was also offered a big money contract to add gloss to the enterprise but turned it down – Greg Norman put a figure on the cash and described Tiger as a 'needle mover'. How much was it?

a) Between $200 and $300 million
b) Between $400 and $500 million
c) Between $700 and $800 million

30 Golf apparel has a reputation for being bland and conservative, governed by the rules and regulations of elite country clubs and staid private member courses. But this wasn't always the way. In the 18th and 19th centuries, when golf was often played on common land, male golfers wore brightly coloured jackets to warn walkers they might be sending dangerous flying golf balls in their direction. True or False?

31 If you rolled up at the 19th hole and ordered an 'Arnold Palmer' what kind of drink would you be expecting?

a) A shot of tequila with a generous splash of soda, lemonade and ice
b) Iced tea mixed in equal parts with lemonade

32 Not to be outdone by one of golf's true legends, John Daly has got his own drink, too, and it's available in a can. John Daly's Hard Tea is an alcoholic mixture of lemonade, iced tea, and vodka. True or False?

33 Dustin Johnson is married to the dazzling Paulina Gretzky. Paulina's dad, Wayne, is considered by many as the G.O.A.T. at which sport?

a) Basketball
b) Baseball
c) Ice Hockey
d) NASCAR

34 Wyndham Clark studied at Oklahoma University and Oregon University before turning pro in 2017. How many tour wins had he managed before his US Open Win at the Los Angeles Country Club in 2023?

a) One
b) Three
c) Six

35 David Feherty has found great fame for his on-course broadcasts, previously for CBS and now on the LIV golf tour. He has also written four books on golf – three of the titles below are genuine, spot the fake.

a) *Somewhere in Ireland a Village is Missing an Idiot*
b) *An Idiot for All Seasons*
c) *David Feherty's Totally Subjective History of the Ryder Cup*
d) *Finding Phil Mickelson* – the rollercoaster ride that is Team Phil

36 On a flight to the States in 1966, psychedelic musician Syd Barrett sat next to Ray Floyd and was impressed by the golfer's 'groovy' pink trousers (man). At the time his band included Roger Waters, Nick Mason and Richard Wright and were known as the 'Tea Set' but were looking for a more original name. When he got back to London, Syd told them what it would be: Pink Floyd. True or False?

37 As we mentioned earlier in the book, there have never been more beards on the professional tour. So who is this popular beardy golfer?

a) Andrew Johnston
b) Tyrrell Hatton
c) Shane Lowry

38 There are seasonal variations and weekly variations in green fees – with a premium at the weekends etc. Which course charges the highest green fee in the US?

a) Pebble Beach, California
b) Shadow Creek, Las Vegas
c) TPC Sawgrass, Florida

39 And which course charges the highest green fee in the UK?

a) St Andrews Old Course
b) Trump Turnberry
c) The Belfry, Brabazon Course

40 Pilgrim's Nook is unique in golf. This nine-hole Pennsylvania course is the only one run by the Amish community. It can be played by non-Amish players, but only hickory-shafted clubs may be used, carried in a bag – no buggies or trolleys. Dress code is plain colours with a degree of leniency exercised, but there is one stipulation that cannot be dodged. All adult male players must have a beard. True or False?

41 The Official Golf World Rankings came under sustained criticism from LIV golf professionals in October 2023, as they watched their OGWR positions slide into treble figures. Only the results achieved in open competitions were being counted and none of the LIV events. What reason did boss Peter Dawson give for excluding them from the calculations?

a) They needed to play big-boy 72-hole events
b) It was a closed competition with only 48 of the 8000+ professionals allowed to play and no cut after two rounds.

42 Icelandic golf are forging an unusual kind of golf course. Led by golf course architect Edwin Roald they are laying out courses with how many holes?

a) 12
b) 15
c) 22 (the original number at St Andrews}

43 Lexi Thompson became only the 7th woman to compete in a PGA tournament in 2023 when she entered the Shriner's Children's Open (for adults) in Las Vegas. How did she get on?

a) She missed the 36-hole cut by three strokes
b) She missed the 36-hole cut by six strokes

44 Which Ryder Cup player pulled out of a practice round at Wentworth in 1992 after he was bitten on the finger by an adder?

a) David Feherty
b) Sam Torrance
c) Bernard Gallacher

45 Golfers like to invest in other sporting franchises. Rory McIlroy is pictured here at the Formula 1 United States Grand Prix with which team?

a) Alpine
b) Haas
c) McLaren

46 As a patriotic Scot Sean Connery spent many of his latter years on the golf course. But growing up in working class Edinburgh he had hardly picked up a golf club until the film *Goldfinger*, for which he was given golf lessons from Peter Alliss. True or False?

41

45

ANSWERS

EAST COURSE

Hole 1: Name That Golf Course – North America

1. Streamsong Golf Resort, Florida
2. Shadow Creek, Las Vegas, Nevada
3. Harbour Town Links, South Carolina
4. Ocean Course, Kiawah Island, South Carolina
5. Oakmont Country Club, Pennsylvania
6. TPC Sawgrass, Florida
7. Pacific Dunes, Oregon
8. Arrowhead Golf Course, Colorado
9. Fairmont Banff Springs Golf Course, Alberta, Canada
10. Augusta National Golf Course, Georgia
11. Chambers Bay, Washington
12. Pebble Beach, California
13. Waikolua, Kauai, Hawaii
14. Whistling Straits, Wisconsin
15. Torrey Pines, California
16. Whistler Golf Club, British Columbia, Canada
17. Moab Golf Course, Utah
18. Brookline Country Club, Massachusetts

Hole 2: Golfing Nicknames

1. Rory McIlroy
2. Retief Goosen
3. Luis Oosthuizen
4. Craig Stadler
5. Greg Norman
6. Andrew Johnston
7. Phil Mickelson
8. Jack Nicklaus
9. James Joseph Waldorf
10. Arnold Palmer
11. John Daly
12. Ernie Els
13. Fred Couples
14. Colin Montgomerie
15. David Duval
16. Craig Parry
17. Masashi Ozaki
18. Paula Creamer
19. Graeme McDowell
20. Paul Azinger
21. Thomas Trent Weekley
22. Gary Player

Hole 3: Balls

1. c) Wood
2. c) Goose
3. c) 361 yards
4. c) Divinity student
5. True
6. a) BF Goodrich
7. a) 1905
8. a) Penfold Heart
9. False
10. a) Hexagonal dimples
11. c) Yellow
12. c) Titleist ProV1
13. c) 100,000
14. c) 420,000
15. c) Dixon Fire

Hole 4: The Masters

1. a) Boer War
2. b) Shinnecock Hills, New York
3. b) 1934
4. c) Too hot
5. c) Thirty-six
6. a) The green jacket
7. a) Western North Carolina
8. b) The par-3 course
9. b) Friends or family
10. c) Lifetime
11. c) Seve Ballesteros

12. b) Jack Nicklaus (6 times)
13. c) Justin Rose
14. a) Ben Hogan
15. False
16. b) 11th, 12th, 13th
17. c) The Butler Cabin
18. b) Sandy Lyle
19. c) Previous winner (except for consecutive winners)
20. c) Tiger Woods 1997
21. c) Dustin Johnson in 2020
22. b) Fish and chips
23. The par-3 16th
24. False
25. b) Jim Nantz
26. c) Mobile/cell phones

Hole 5: Lefties

1. Right hand
2. a) 1963
3. a) Gerry
4. True
5. b) 'Butcher of Hoylake'
6. b) Mike Weir
7. a) David Feherty
8. True
9. False
10. a) Louis Oosthuizen

Hole 6: Commentator Quotes

1. a) Jack Nicklaus
2. c) Gary McCord
3. a) Gary Player
4. Ken – on the course – Brown

5. b) Jim Furyk
6. c) 'Still your shot'
7. a) Craig Stadler
8. a) Miguel Ángel Jiménez
9. c) John Daly
10. Tiger Woods

Hole 7: Spanish Golfers

1. b) El Niño
2. c) Masters and US Open
3. c) Five
4. b) 137
5. b) Smoking a cigar
6. b) Cantabria
7. True (allegedly)
8. a) Most starts
9. a) Jon Rahm

Hole 3: Balls

Hole 6: Ken on the course with Bernhard Langer

Hole 10: Georgia Hall

Hole 11: The Golden State Warriors' Steph Curry

10. d) Edouard España
11. b) They are Basques
12. Miguel Ángel Jiménez

Hole 8: St Andrews

1. b) 1764
2. a) 1552 – rabbit warren
3. b) Scene of Molinari's famous putt
4. True
5. c) Cameron Smith
6. a) Benjamin Franklin
7. b) His ashes are still there
8. b) 700 years
9. True
10. True
11. a) Zach Johnson
12. c) Ross Fisher

Hole 9: Famous Par-3s

1. a) 1923
2. a) Mourne Mountains
3. b) 24
4. b) 4th
5. c) Barbados
6. a) Arrowhead Point
7. a) The Coliseum
8. a) Pinched Nerve
9. b) Pete Dye
10. c) 248 yards

Hole 10: Women's Golf

1. a) 1893
2. c) Her third tournament
3. d) New Zealander
4. a) 14
5. c) 1976
6. c) Eight

7. b) Ten
8. a) Evian les Bains
9. b) There is no statue at the R&A
10. c) Boyfriend
11. d) Australian
12. True
13. a) Georgia Hall
14. a) Curtis Cup
15. c) Inbee Park
16. a) Nelly Korda
17. c) $101m
18. c) Six holes before the end of the tournament. The incident led to a subsequent change of rules.
19. True
20. c) 1990

Hole 11: Golf-Obsessed Sports Stars

1. a) Steph Curry
2. a) Tommy Fleetwood
3. False
4. True
5. c) Aaron Rodgers
6. a) 5th
7. a) Pete Sampras
8. a) Harry Maguire (sacked Man Utd captain)
9. b) Carlos Sainz
10. a) Patrick Mahomes

Hole 12: Rules, Rules, Rules

1. b) Dropped again
2. a) Knee height
3. c) Two club lengths (but it may well annoy the greenskeeper)
4. a) Three minutes
5. b) 14
6. b) 10 seconds
7. No – you can get a free drop from GUR
8. No
9. Yes. Previously it was necessary for the ball to hit the bottom of the cup, but now if any part is below the surface, it's holed.
10. b) No penalty
11. No. Just lucky. A ball is only considered Out of Bounds when it comes to rest
12. No
13. b)
14. b)
15. b)
16. a) 40 seconds
17. True
18. No. In this situation the ball, which is on the tee, is not in play. It only becomes a ball in play once there is intent, and a deliberate stroke is made.
19. c)
20. Yes

Hole 13: Le Euro Golf

1. a) Le bunker
2. b) Ball
3. b) Mid-irons
4. c) Balle!
5. a) Divot
6. b) It's all square
7. a) Yes, it's a birdie
8. a) Legno (a wood)
9. a) Dress code
10. c) A divot

Hole 14: Water Hazards

1. Rae's Creek
2. a) Play from the beach
3. c) The Barry Burn
4. c) 14. He hit one into a garden and three into the Pacific, giving him an 83. "It's amazing how quickly it went," said Daly's caddie Dan Quinn
5. b) It's the fishing hole
6. a) To the lighthouse
7. c) The PGA estimates 100-120,000
8. a) Act of Parliament
9. a) Ernie Els
10 a) Prestwick

Hole 15: Irish Golfers

1. c) He shot 80
2. a) Accountant
3. c) Ben Crenshaw (who broke his putter and had to use an iron)
4. b) Graeme McDowell
5. b) Ronan Rafferty and Philip Walton
6. His wife had died
7. c) Sergio Garcia
8. c) Royal Portrush
9. Covid-19 prevented the 2020 tournament taking place
10. c) Manchester United
11. a) 2002
12. c) Brother-in-law

Hole 16: The US Open

1. c) -16
2. c) $3.6m
3. c) Jack Nicklaus from 1957–2000
4. a) Shinnecock Hills
5. b) First professional win
6. c) Brookline Country Club

Hole 16: Martin Kaymer

7. c) Oakmont, Pennsylvania
8. a) Scottish
9. c) 1911
10. d) New York
11. b) Brooks Koepka
12. b) Curtis Strange, 1988 and 1989
13. 2000 at Pebble Beach
14. c) Fifteen strokes
15. Yes
16. c) Ten years
17. c) Xander Schauffele
18. b) Martin Kaymer in 2014
19. b) A Volkswagen Beetle
20. True. In 2051 the US Open will be held at Oakland Hills, Michigan

Hole 17: Golfers' Quotes

1. John Daly
2. Bobby Jones
3. Jack Nicklaus
4. Tiger Woods
5. Bernhard Langer
6. Lee Trevino
7. Rory Mcilroy
8. Arnold Palmer
9. Patrick Reed
10. Gary Player
11. Seve Ballesteros
12. Patrick Reed
13. Tom Watson
14. Colin Montgomerie
15. Ian Poulter
16. Max Faulkner
17. Jean van de Velde
18. Phil Mickelson
19. Patrick Cantlay
20. Greg Norman

Hole 18: Name That Golf Course – Scotland

1. Turnberry
2. Loch Lomond
3. Gleneagles
4. Castle Stuart/Cabot
5. Lundin Ladies
6. Isle of Barra
7. Isle of Harris
8. Royal Troon
9. Kingsbarns
10. North Berwick
11. St Andrews
12. Carnoustie

Hole 18 Dogleg: Name That Golf Course – Ireland

1. Tralee Golf Club
2. Royal Portrush
3. Ballyliffin
4. Castle Dromoland
5. Head of Kinsale
6. Royal County Down
7. Lahinch
8. The K Club

Hole 17: Jean van de Velde

WEST COURSE

Hole 1: Unusual Golfing Hazards

1. b) Little bells
2. a) Children and teenagers
3. a) The Heatstroke Open
4. b) Fisherman
5. c) Pepper spray
6. c) Arctic tern
7. b) Lake Panic
8. a) Bull sharks
9. b) Snake
10. b) Rio
11. False (Skippy the Bush Kangaroo reference)
12. a) Two putts (no matter how close to the pin)

Hole 2: The Ryder Cup

1. a) He was a seed salesman
2. b) Dai Rees
3. b) Sergio Garcia
4. b) Jordan Spieth: 21 years, 1 month, 30 days
5. a) Ray Floyd
6. a) Jon Rahm
7. b) Jack Nicklaus
8. a) Brian Barnes
9. No
10. a) 1979
11. Mark James and Ken Brown
12. Stewart Cink
13. a) Reed and Spieth
14. c) Seve and José María
15. b) Valderrama
16. c) Max Homa
17. b) 1971
18. c) 1985
19. True
20. c) Justin Leonard
21. b) 2014
22. a) Hovland & Aberg
23. c) Viktor was on his own
24. d) Sergio Garcia
25. a) Medinah

Hole 3: Name That Golf Course – Rest of the World

1. Merapi
2. Bangkok Golf Resort
3. Gloria Golf Club
4. Emirates Golf Course
5. Meknes Golf Club
6. Kau Sai Chau

Hole 1: In Australia, the water is just the start of the hazard

Hole 4: Name That Golfer

1. Minji Lee
2. Paula Creamer
3. Brooke Henderson
4. Nelly Korda
5. Georgia Hall
6. Hyunju Yoo
7. Atthaya Thitkul
8. Inbee Park
9. Annika Sörenstam
10. Lydia Ko
11. Michell Wie
12. Celine Boutier
13. Lexi Thompson
14. Beatriz Recari

Hole 5: Amazing Holes

1. a) Ferry
2. c) Hunan province
3. True
4. a) Seven
5. b) River island green
6. True
7. a) Ancient Britons
8. At one stage playing golf was banned in Wales but allowed in England
9. a) Standing stones
10. b) 400 yards

Hole 6: Australian Golfers

1. c) Chris Evert
2. a) 2023 US Open
3. a) 6' (183cm)
4. c) Tiger Woods
5. b) Steve Elkington
6. a) Western Australians
7. c) Minjee Lee
8. True
9. b) Fred Couples
10. b) Grass pollen
11. d) Peter Thomson
12. c) Nine

Hole 7: Name That Golf Course – Australia & New Zealand

1. Cape Kidnappers
2. Queenstown Golf Club
3. Rotorua
4. Barnbougle
5. Cape Wickham
6. Royal Melbourne
7. Rottnest Island (home of the Quokka)
8. Jack's Point

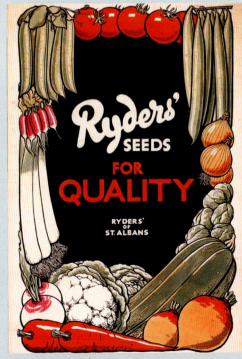

Hole 2: Samuel Ryder's seed company catalogue

Hole 2: The inimitable Brian Barnes

Hole 8: Mavericks

1. True. Seve Ballesteros, commentating on the BBC, said that would be the closest he'd get to the Claret Jug.
2. True
3. c) The irreplaceable Brian Barnes
4. a) 1999
5. b) Built his own course
6. c) Bryson deChambeau
7. c) Mark James
8. a) Third
9. a) 1980
10. b) Australian rugby league players with mullets

Hole 9: Chokes and Blunders

1. c) 78
2. c) One
3. a) Nick Faldo
4. c) Bob Goalby
5. b) Yes
6. True
7. b) Jack Nicklaus
8. a) Padraig Harrington
9. a) Geoff Ogilvy
10. c) Photo shows one of Thomas Bjørn's failed escapes

Hole 10: World Famous Bunkers

1. a) Spectacles
2. b) Hell Bunker
3. c) San Andreas Fault
4. Yes
5. b) Chambers Bay
6. c) 13,000
7. a) Chicago
8. a) The Church Pews
9. a) Out of Bounds
10. b) Himalaya
11. a) The Cape Bunker
12. Postage Stamp, Royal Troon

Hole 11: The Open Championship

1. c) Twenty-nine
2. b) Musselburgh
3. c) Belt – as modelled by Young Tom Morris
4. a) Stewart Cink
5. b) Eight

Hole 11: Young Tom Morris with belt

Hole 17: Sir Nick reunited with Fanny at the 150th Open

6. a) Justin Leonard
7. a) Royal St George's
8. c) 396
9. a) Padraig Harrington
10. b) 1976
11. c) The Capitol Riots
12. a) Constantino Rocca
13. c) Prestwick
14. b) Bunker free
15. Alex
16. b) Nine
17. c) Henrik Stenson – 264
18. c) Until the age of 60
19. b) Mark Calcavecchia
20. The Open must be played on a links course
21. True
22. a) Forty-three – and the defending champion missed the cut
23. Jack Nicklaus
24. a) Jack Nicklaus – seven times
25. The Vardon grip

Hole 12: Innovations in Golf

1. a) Ash and hazel – hickory came later
2. b) Graphite shafts
3. b) Putter
4. a) Franklin Grant
5. True
6. b) Gene Sarazen
7. c) Prince of Wales
8. a) Big Bertha
9. a) Ping
10. a) Frank Stableford

Hole 13: Name That Golf Course - Europe

1. Dunstanburgh Castle
2. Chamonix
3. Vale do Lobo
4. Biarritz
5. Brautarhalt
6. Budersand Sylt
7. Rome
8. Tenerife
9. Lofoten Islands
10. Le Touquet
11. Valderrama
12. Harlech
13. Crete
14. Etretat
15. Tranrüs, Dolomites
16. Crans-sur-Sierre
17. Bro Hof Slott
18. Alcanada

Hole 14: No.1 in the World

1. b) 25
2. a) Faldo, Norman, Woods
3. c) Scotland
4. a) Tom Lehman
5. b) Bernhard Langer
6. c) 281 weeks
7. a) Lee Westwood
8. b) Northern Ireland
9. c) 8000+
10. c) Ernie Els

Hole 15: South African Golfers

1. b) 6'8"
2. c) 52

3. Gary Player (though he was married for 64 years)
4. True
5. a) Masters
6. c) Ernie Els
7. False
8. a) Savannah
9. a) Theodore
10. c) 78.7 – The highest for a final U.S. Open round since 1972 at Pebble Beach.

Hole 16: The Hole Name

1. Augusta National
2. St Andrews
3. Spyglass Hill
4. Tralee
5. Dinard
6. Machrihanish
7. Royal Troon
8. Hoylake
9. Shinnecock Hills
10. Carnoustie

Hole 17: Caddies

1. b) From cadet
2. b) Ten per cent
3. True
4. a) Alex (in the days when he was little)
5. True
6. Lydia Ko
7. c) 1976
8. Nick Faldo
9. True
10. a) Adam Scott

Hole 19: The Amish do play softball and volleyball

Hole 19: John Daly's trousers (see page 178) help promote his drinks brand

Hole 18: The Way They Were

1. Patrick Reed
2. Rickie Fowler
3. Jon Rahm
4. Tyrrell Hatton
5. Shane Lowry
6. Jordan Spieth
7. Daniel* Willett
8. Cameron Smith
9. Ian Poulter
10. Matt Fitzpatrick
11. Scottie Scheffler
12. Viktor Hovland
13. Dustin Johnson
14. Brian Harman
15. Rory McIlroy
16. Brooks Koepka

* as he was then known to Getty Images caption writers

**19th Hole: Dodgy Bounces
and Tricky Lies**
1. True
2. True
3. True. Philadelphia Cricket
   Club
4. b) The Devil's Butt
5. c) Tony Jacklin CBE
6. c) Pine tree removed
7. a) 2.8
8. False. George H.W. Bush
   had the lower handicap
9. c) Golf investors
10. b) Apollo 14
11. c) 40 yards
12. a) Lee Trevino
13. c) £ to $
14. False. And the photo is
    of professional golfer

Sophie Lamb
15. c) Condor
16. b) Billy Horschel
17. True
18. c) *Full Swing*
19. a) Curlew
20. a) Pillbox
21. False
22. True. St Enodoc church is
    entirely surrounded by
    the golf course
23. True
24. c) Spending time with his
    tractor
25. False
26. c)
27. a) Selling cups of tea
28. c) Kit-Kat
29. c) $700-800m

30. True
31. b) Iced tea
32. True
33. c) Ice hockey
34. a) One
35. d) *Finding Phil Mickelson*
36. False
37. c) Shane Lowry
38. b) Shadow Creek, Las
    Vegas
39. b) Trump Turnberry
40. False. Sadly, there is no
    such course
41. b) Closed entry
42. a) 12
43. a) Three strokes
44. a) David Feherty
45. a) Alpine
46. True

PICTURE CREDITS

All photos courtesy of Shutterstock with the following exceptions:
Brautarholt Golf Club, p147 (middle), 172 (top)
Peter Drew/Unsplash.com, p20 (middle right), 62 (top)
Frank Hopkinson, p112 (top), 113
The K Club, p89 (bottom)
Library of Congress, p23 (bottom left), 166, 188 (left)
Meadow Farms Golf Club, p111
Evangelos Mpkikas/Unsplash.com, p151 (top right)
Oakmont Country Club, p11 (bottom)
Dean Ricciardi/Unsplash.com, p132 (middle)
Royal County Down Golf Club, p45 (middle)
Sandy Lane Golf Course, p45 (bottom)
Tralee Golf Club, p88 (left)
Trump Turnberry, p47 (top)

Getty Images, p7, 10 (top), 12 (top, middle), 15 (bottom), 16, 17 (top), 19 (bottom), 23 (bottom right), 31 (top right), 31 (bottom), 32, 34, 35, 37 (bottom right), 39 (bottom), 41 (left), 45 (top), 51 (top left), 53 (top), 55 (bottom right), 58, 64 (top), 69, 71, 73 (bottom), 75, 78, 79, 81 (middle left, bottom left), 83 (top left, bottom left), 88 (middle right, bottom right), 89 (middle left), 94 (top), 97 (bottom), 98 (bottom left), 101, 102 (bottom left, bottom right, middle right), 108 (top right), 110 (bottom), 112 (bottom), 116, 117, 118 (bottom), 121, 123, 125, 126, 127, 130, 131 (top, middle), 132 (bottom), 134, 135, 136, 137, 139, 140, 141, 142, 143, 145, 146, 148, 149, 150 (middle), 154, 157 (top), 158, 159, 161 (left, bottom right), 162 (top), 163, 164, 165, 169, 171, 174 (bottom), 178, 179, 181 (right), 182 (bottom), 187 (right), 188 (right).

ALSO AVAILABLE...

ISBN 9780711286443

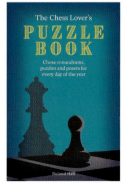

ISBN 9780711289840

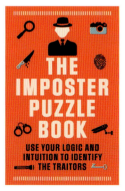

ISBN 9780711289871

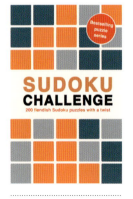

ISBN 9780711290686

ISBN 9780711290662

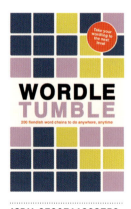

ISBN 9780711282759

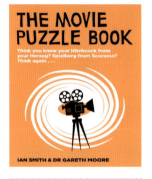

ISBN 9780711286634

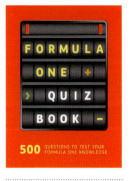

ISBN 9780711286474